THE ANATOMY
OF
FRUSTRATION

Discover How to Transform Frustration into Creative
Opportunities & Unlock the Power to Succeed

RICHARD ONEBAMOI

The ROCK Publishing
Brussels, Belgium

Unless otherwise indicated, all scripture quotations are taken from the King James Version of the Bible.

Anatomy of Frustration: Discover how to transform frustration into creative opportunities and unlock the power to succeed

Copyright © 2008 by Richard Onebamoi

ISBN 978-908126360-3
D/2008/11789/3

Personal Development, Self-Improvement, Success, Empowerment, Motivation, Self-Help

Richard Onebamoi International
P.O. Box 30
1200 Brussels
Belgium
E-mail: info@richardonebamoi.com
Websites: www.richardonebamoibooks.com; www.richardonebamoi.com.

Published by The ROCK Publishing
Richard Onebamoi
P.O. Box 30
1200 Brussels
Belgium

Printed in Belgium

Join My Reader's List

Signup for notification of new books by
Richard Onebamoi and exclusive giveaway.

https://www.richardonebamoibooks.com/

Your Free Gift

As a way of saying thank you for purchasing, I am offering a special free report Frustration-Proof Your Life that reveals everything you need to know about how to put a stop to your anxiety and depression and to unlock the power to succeed.

Sign up today to claim yours
FRUSTRATION-PROOF REPORT

https://www.richardonebamoibooks.com/freereport/

DEDICATION

I wish to dedicate this book to Angela Onebamoi, my beloved sister, an extraordinary woman of faith, and one of the most loving people I ever knew. You believed in me when no one else did. You were an inspiration to everyone who knew you. I only wish you could be here to enjoy the fruit of your labor. You left us too soon.

Adieu, Sister.

ACKNOWLEDGMENTS

I want to thank my beloved wife, Catherine, who always makes valuable suggestions for my books and who, as part of my life, has made the releasing of my potential and fulfilling my purpose a worthwhile journey of success.

I want to say a heartfelt thank you to our wonderful children; Naomi-Lisha, Nearia-Destinie, Nathania-Mia, and Nathan-Richard, for continuing to allow me to go into the wee hours of the night to put the thoughts of this book together.

I wish to thank all of the wonderful vessels of God who have been a source of great inspiration and encouragement and from whom I have learned a lot over the years.

TABLE OF CONTENTS

* * * * * *

INTRODUCTION

Frustration is an observable fact that you have to deal with daily. The burdens of work, family, unforeseen crises, and unmet expectations combine to produce tangled loops of the frustrating events in your life. When you are frustrated, your mind cannot work efficiently. Instead of focusing on possibilities, your mind focuses on impossibilities, and your thoughts are not coherent at this stage.

While there are certain things that you can do to make your life run more smoothly, we must also understand that, as a human, you have limitations just like anybody else that will incapacitate you, causing things not to run as smoothly as you would desire. This makes frustrating situations inevitable as you progress and navigate through the corridors of life.

Frustration in life is not only inevitable but also useful. However, what you choose to do or not to do in moments of frustration is what will determine your ability to do that which is necessary to achieve the expected end and your inability to produce your desired outcome. It is not what you go through that ultimately determines your outcome, but how you respond to the events responsible for the frustration.

Jack Canfield has formulated a blueprint that I think drives this point home: Events + Response = Outcome (E+R=O). If you do not appreciate the outcome, such as frustration, in your life, all you need to do is to change your response to the events until you get the anticipated outcome.

The initial reaction of most people to frustration is often to succumb to its negative consequences without taking action in the direction of their anticipated outcome. You are either resisting or ignoring it altogether, putting up a protective defense and confronting it as an enemy with which you feel you must do battle. Yielding, resisting, ignoring partially or completely this emotional disposition and others like it, is disadvantageous and can only produce negative results. You will find yourself producing more frustration, anxiety, stress, and fear than opportunities, possibilities, and the power to succeed.

In times of frustration, you need to ask the right kind of questions, which will empower you to take action in the right direction about the problem and the condition at hand. Frustration has been considered as an unnecessary evil responsible for your demise. To a larger extent, it has prevailed as such, but this book will open your eyes to see beyond your present conditions, crystallizing the anatomy of frustration in clear terms and how you can transform frustration, see opportunities, possibilities, and unlock your power to succeed. Having the proper perspective of frustration is vitally important in achieving tremendous results.

You will grow to become an outstanding example of an achievement that will negate the supposed negative effects of frustration. Frustration actually can be a valuable tool for achieving some of your greatest achievements. Anthony Robbins, one of the experts on personal and human development has this to say:

"I've come to believe that all my past failure and frustrations were actually laying the foundation for the understandings that have created the new level of living I now enjoy." This is not just true for Mr. Robbins but equally true for anyone that will learn and apply these simple strategies detailed in this book.

There are limitless possibilities and positive advantages to this emotional trauma. Ralph Marston explains: "You've done it before and you can do it now. See the positive possibilities. Redirect the substantial energy of your frustration and turn it into positive, effective, unstoppable determination." This could not be more accurate. All you need to do is to decide that you will become unstoppable. Become determined to harness the energy of frustration, transforming it into extraordinary opportunities, and unlocking the power to succeed in any endeavor.

Pope John XXIII said: "Consult not your fears but your hopes and your dreams. Think not about your frustrations, but about your unfulfilled potential. Concern yourself not with what you tried and failed in, but with what it is still possible for you to do." This is a great antidote to frustration in your personal and professional life. When you develop the right kind of mental processes, and you concern yourself with the positive possibilities, you will become unstoppable.

This is not a book about techniques, but about real-life issues that have seen many wonderful people destroyed to come up short of their potential and purpose. It's about discovering the simple yet profound strategies that apply to anyone in any given situation for transforming frustration into productive opportunities and unlocking the power to succeed. One of the ideas that I have developed in this book is that there are always lessons to learn amid challenges and frustrating situations. Discerning and focusing on those lessons are paramount to turning frustrating situations into opportunities that can create the life you have always dreamt of and the kind of person you have always wanted to be.

Richard Onebamoi

PART I

THE ANATOMY
OF FRUSTRATION

CHAPTER 1
WHAT IS FRUSTRATION?

"One of the sources of pride in being a human being is the ability to bear present frustrations in the interests of longer purposes."

Helen Merell Lynd

Anatomy Defined

There are different definitions of anatomy. However, the one that best illustrates the anatomy of the main subject of this book is "the examination of what something is like, the way it works, and why it happens. It is a detailed analysis of something." Consequently, in applying that definition to the subject matter, it reads:

"Anatomy of frustration is the detailed analysis of what frustration is, the way it works, and why it happens."

This implies taking a critical look at frustration for what it is, examining its merits, demerits, and how to objectively address it to transform it into creative opportunities and unlocking the power to succeed. With this understanding, we can now begin to explore in proper perspective this emotional dysfunction called frustration.

Frustration Defined

Frustration (from Dictionary.com): a feeling of dissatisfaction, often accompanied by anxiety or depression, resulting from unfulfilled needs or unresolved problems.

Frustration (from Merriam Webster Dictionary): 1. The act of frustrating. 2. The state or an instance of being frustrated; a deep chronic sense or state of insecurity and dissatisfaction arising from unresolved problems or unfulfilled needs. 3. Something that frustrates

Frustration Also Can Be Defined As:
  » Feeling of disappointment, discomfort, or defeat at being unable to accomplish one's purpose or goals
  » A feeling of dissatisfaction that results when your expectations are not realized
  » Frustration stemming out of hopelessness, fear, anxiety, failure, and desperation
  » A feeling of annoyance at being hindered or criticized
  » Anger produced by some annoying irritation
  » Being prevented from attaining a purpose

Your inability to begin or continue mental processes, often attributed to emotional stress, can also be termed as frustration. You have suffered from frustration one time or another and able to effectively address it is essential for your personal and professional development. This can be a decisive factor between success and failure in any undertaking. Frustration occurs in situations where one is obstructed or prevented from reaching a personal or professional goal. The more important the goals tend to be, the more intense the frustration. Suffice to say there are levels of frustrations. However, no matter its level, frustration must be addressed to avoid devastation.

People react differently to frustration. Some people are completely turned off from the situation, while others continue with something else. There are also those that become incapacitated by their frustration.

Frustration can have an extremely damaging impact on your psychological state, attitude, focus, or mood at a particular time; it can slow down your progress and ultimately immobilize you. You see, what you do not confront today will live on to confront you another day. Hence, it is to your advantage to address or to seek help with the issue and leverage the support of others when frustration occurs.

Despite all of the reasons why you have failed to achieve your goals, acquire outstanding results, and live the life of your dreams. There is one cause that is now prevalent in the 21st-century frustration with a capital F. To achieve your goals; you must learn to transform frustration into creative opportunities and harness the energy to unlock the power to succeed. Frustration ranks high among many other emotional dysfunctions. It cannot be overlooked any longer, as the outcome will be devastating. However, if you meet your resolve with determination, the rewards will be enormous.

Anthony Robbins argues that "people who fail to achieve their goals usually get stopped by frustration. They allow frustration to keep them from taking the necessary actions that would support them in achieving their desire. You get through this roadblock by plowing through frustration, taking each setback as the feedback you can learn from, and pushing ahead. I doubt you'll find many successful people who have not experienced this. All successful people learn that success is buried on the other side of frustration." For that reason, to leverage frustration as a resource, you have to change how you view it. This will eliminate the possibility of unproductiveness.

One of the greatest frustrations in life is that which comes from feeling out of control and powerless. You feel intense frustration over unaccomplished goals and struggle with issues that you are unable to control, for instance, how the weather turns out today or tomorrow or how people respond to you or unable to the control traffic on your way to the office or your lack of ability to control the overall outcome of a business event. Studies have shown that 7 of 10 people are affected by frustration; three are severely affected. This is alarming.

There are things in life that will be out of your control. Coming to terms with this will help transform your frustration into creative opportunities that can yield amazing results. For instance, you can gain an incredible amount of information by listening to an audiobook in your car to distract you from your inability to control the traffic.

Our world today has become highly competitive and technologically advanced, which has led to situations where most people sets goals to be achieved within a given time frame if they must stay relevant to the trends of times. When these personal or professional goals are not achieved, frustration sets in. The objectives were not met, which results in frustration, stress, and lack of motivation. Understanding that situations like these are temporal and not final is key to keeping your head above the waters of frustration.

The feeling of frustration can affect the mind in such a way that it could be empowering or disempowering depending on the line of action pursued. Your thinking prowess will be hindered gravely if that individual's perspective is negative. Having the right perspective can help translate your frustration into creative opportunities, possibilities, and personal fulfillment.

Countless situations have led people to make erroneous decisions, resulting in their inability to come up with innovative ideas. For instance, Nathan Jones, a CEO of a leading fortune 500 firms, noticed that he was becoming overweight. He set a goal to lose 10kg within a month but lost only 2kg. As a result, he became unmotivated and allowed his frustration to mar his thinking ability that would have helped him come up with innovative ideas for his current situation or seek assistance with his goal. This is what will occur when you allow frustration to have a negative impact.

How Frustration Can Affect You

Frustration can affect you spiritually, emotionally, mentally, and physically. It can affect your ability to make decisions congruent with your core values. It can affect your relationships with your loved ones, colleagues, and acquaintances. Frustration can also affect your outlook on life by distorting what is most important to you. Frustration that is left unattended for one reason or another can also affect your health. It can impede the full manifestation of your potential. It is, therefore, imperative to examine how you are affected by frustration. Make a note and take action immediately to translate anything negative into a positive and unlock the power to succeed.

Here are a few key points to consider

» Have the right perspective of the situation.

» Define and set realistic expectations and achievable goals.

» Understand that there are things you cannot control.

Have the Right Perspective: This is very important as you deal with everyday life issues. Occasionally, you have been astonished at yourself and the aftermath of the decisions you made, because you did not have the right perspective. No matter the circumstance, take the time to evaluate, seek wise counsel, and think through each situation. This process will bring clarity to some things and allow you to have insight into what is working and what is not.

Set Realistic Expectations and Achievable Goals: Expectations or goals that aren't realistic could be the major reason for your frustration. Do not go off on a tangent. Set goals that are congruent with your core values, not someone else's, and make use of the resources at your disposal. This does not mean that you should not stretch yourself beyond what seems impossible but should not be overstated —this will do you more harm than good. For instance, a goal to build a thriving business within six months is not likely to be achieved. To avoid frustration, you must learn to set realistic goals.

Understand that There are Things Beyond Your Control: Several events are occurring in your life that cause a great deal of frustration. To be candid, sometimes it's not necessarily the events responsible for your frustration but your inability to control the outcome. I cannot stress this enough: You have to realize that there are things you cannot control. To know this will help you deal with frustration. You must understand that there are situations that are beyond your control. This has nothing to do with strengths or weaknesses but just the simple fact that you are human.

Are you on the verge of a nervous breakdown at work, at home, or considering giving up on your dreams? Of course, these are challenges pertinent to everyone, and you are not alone in this life process. It is evident that some of our expectations are not easy to achieve, but they are not impossible, either. That's why you must hold on to your dreams until they come to fruition. It's the process of making your goals happen that gives you a reason to rejoice.

Nido Qubein remarked, "When a goal matters enough to a person, that person will find a way to accomplish what at first seemed impossible." Impossible situations are things or events which have not been achieved before; of course, this does not negate the possibilities of accomplishing those things or events. Remain determined and follow through on your commitments to transform your frustrations into creative opportunities and unlock your power to succeed. Where we're going next is to identify the *roots of frustration.*

CHAPTER 2

ROOTS OF FRUSTRATION

"Frustration, although quite painful at times, is a very positive and essential part of success."

Bo Bennett

The root cause of frustration is multifarious. Frustration produces anger, resentment, bitterness, apathy, discontentment, indisposition, regret, weariness, and hatred. These emotions have an object that triggers them. Sometimes our ambitions exceed our abilities, or we misperceive the possibilities, resulting in unmet expectations, which ultimately produce frustration.

It is often said that you manage frustration. I believe that you never master anything you manage. Instead of managing frustration, identify its roots, and deal with it from that perspective. When you address the issue of frustration from the root, it produces more lasting and positive results over time.

Frustration may be internal or external. Internal frustration involves personal deficiencies such as lack of confidence, low self-esteem, or fear of social situations that prevent goal achievement. Internal conflict can also result in frustration when one has conflicting goals. The story of the Apostle Paul is a good example. He said, "For that which I do I allow not: for what I would, that do I not; but what I hate that I do" (Romans 7:15). Out of frustration, he cried out, "O wretched man that I am! Who shall deliver me from the body of this death?" Romans 7:24 External frustration involves outside conditions such as an external event that is beyond your immediate control and creates extreme demand like insubordinate colleagues or blocked roads.

We will examine some of the root causes of frustration, which will also demystify notions that have been purported in recent times, such as that frustration is a necessary evil. Frustration is common to all of us and occurs in various degrees. No one is immune to this feeling, but how you respond to it is what sets winners apart from losers.

Sources of Frustration

Complexities of Everyday Life: A "complex" in the context of personal and professional development can be defined as "a system of interrelated, emotion-charged ideas, feelings, memories, and impulses that may be repressed but continues to influence thoughts and behavior" (Dictionary.com). We are often overwhelmed by the complex situations of everyday life. These situations can affect your focus and drain your spiritual energy, which will hinder you in pursuit of your destiny. Complexities in personal and professional life are common to all of us, but it is how you address these issues that help you unlock the power to succeed in any endeavor.

Complex situations are nothing but a series of unresolved situations or intertwined events that form a myriad of things in our lives. It is just like a web that a spider creates: it begins with a single thread that turns into a cobweb. Unfortunately, if these complex situations are not resolved, they can create terrible frustration, anger, and disappointment that will have short- and long-term consequences. Your success is at risk if you believe that complex situations are impossible to resolve. Therefore, to deal with a complex situation, you must first adjust and realign your attitude with your overall objective. There will always be complex situations in your life; to think to the contrary would be naïve. Aim to understand the complex situation through research, evaluation, and a mastermind alliance. Liberate yourself of procrastination by taking immediate action to resolve any issue to avoid the accumulation of unresolved situations.

Lack of Faith: What is faith? The Bible says that "Now faith is the substance of things hoped for, the evidence of things not seen" (Hebrews 11:1). It is the ability to reach beyond yourself, to go past the obvious circumstances that surround you. You can become convinced of the reality of things that you have not yet seen. It enables you to anticipate things that are not yet noticeable to the natural senses. Sherwood Eddy said, "Faith is not trying to believe something regardless of the evidence. Faith is daring to do something, regardless of the consequence." This is the foremost root cause of frustration. When you take an honest look at the issues that bring about this frustration, you discover it is nothing but a lack of faith in God concerning the situation, event, or even the relationship.

In 2 Corinthians 5.7, we read: "For we walk by faith, not by sight." The word "walk" is of interest because the actual rendering in the Greek means *to regulate one's life or to conduct oneself.* In other words, you regulate your life or conduct yourself by faith and not by what you see or perceive in the natural world. Your plans may be frustrating because it is simply not His will. Helen Keller said that "optimism is the faith that leads to achievement. Nothing can be done without hope and confidence." When you have this perspective, you will be able to identify frustration as a possibility and translate it into something productive.

Unfulfilled Expectations: Unfulfilled expectations are often the root cause of frustrations in your personal or professional life. Most people that I know have one or more expectations at any given time; when these expectations are unmet or unfulfilled, frustration often results. For instance, when you have established goals to be achieved within a time frame, and you are unable to achieve these goals, this leads to frustration, anger, and disappointment.

You have expectations from your spouse, boss, colleagues, friends, and acquaintances. When these expectations are not met, frustration will likely arise. What you must do is step back, re-evaluate your expectations, and make adjustments where necessary. Solicit feedback to allow you to ascertain what is and isn't working. Focus on your expectations, not on the frustration. On occasion, you will have to communicate your expectations to those that are involved. You cannot keep doing the same thing over and over again, expecting a different result. You may have to change your actions that will produce the anticipated outcome.

Most importantly, you have to stay the course. Do not allow frustration to deny you of your birthright. Don't give up, and don't give in.

Lack of Direction: Henry David Thoreau said, "If one advances confidently in the direction of one's dreams, and endeavors to live the life which one has imagined, one will meet with a success unexpected in common hours." According to Jim Rohn, "You cannot change your destination overnight, but you can change your direction overnight." You must have a clear road map at every step of your task because lack of direction will lead to uncompleted or haphazardly completed tasks. Without direction, you will not know when you will arrive at your desired objective, and you will not be able to repeat the process.

Lack of direction will lead to frustration when meaningful results are not obtained. At home with your loved ones or at work with your colleagues, you must define your objectives, what you intend to achieve in the relationship, and how you intend to achieve it. Without these steps, there will be a misunderstanding, indifference, and, ultimately, frustration. Use this technique before and after you embark on your task, as this will help you leverage all of the resources at your disposal when frustrating circumstances occur.

Failure: Sooner or later, every human being that breathes comes across failure in some shape or form. Law of Human Behavior states, "Sooner or later we will get what we expect." This law is explicit enough. What you expect is going to be your reality. For example, if you expect to fail sooner or later, you will fail. Every situation is education. No one enjoys failing, but it's inevitable. For example, Mr. Jobson performed poorly on his driver's permit test and failed. This was neither his first nor his second test; as a result of the fact that he failed to reach his objectives, he was frustrated and disappointed.

Failure to achieve one's desires or expectations can result in frustration and can affect you in very remarkable ways. However, failure is one of the breakfasts of champions. Individuals who have never failed are those who haven't done anything. It is imperative to understand that failure is not a destination but an event that occurs in pursuit of your goals and objectives. As Rogier Von Oech puts it, "there are two benefits of failure. First, if you do fail, you learn what doesn't work; and second, the failure gives you an opportunity to try a new approach... Most people think of success and failure as opposites, but they are both products of the same process."

Lack of Control: The truth of the matter is that life is filled with things that become frustrating; certainly, most of these things are out of your control. Lack of control is one of the root causes of frustration. Charles Popplestown states, "You cannot always control circumstances, but you can control your own thoughts." This problem is quite common but not obvious. First and foremost, recognize that you have no control over things around you, but you do have control over how you respond to those frustrating events that occur in your life.

Kelsey Grammer remarked, "The mark of a man is one who knows he can't control his circumstances— but he can control his responses." A lot of people get extremely frustrated because they cannot control a situation to their advantage. Given the fact that there is a lack of control, a feeling of disappointment, exasperation, or weariness takes over, producing anger, stress, or resentment. These individuals do not realize that there are circumstances in life that we cannot control for the simple fact that we are human.

Jim Rohn is often quoted as saying that "it is the set of the sails, not the direction of the wind that determines which way we will go." To be frustrated at the direction of the wind, which is beyond your control, is unproductive. It is, therefore, imperative to understand that one may not be able to control certain situations or events because they do not depend on you directly or indirectly. You need to learn how to let go of some of the things with which you are struggling; when that happens is when you gain.

The habit of Quitting: Ross Perot remarked, "Most people give up just when they are about achieving success. They quit on the one-yard line. They give up at the last minute of the game, one foot from a winning touchdown." Vince Lombardi observed, "Once you learn to quit, it becomes a habit." This could not be more accurate. One of the root causes of frustration is the habit of quitting when overtaken by temporary defeat, setback, or detour.

Most people tend to quit when they encounter setbacks because they did not achieve their desired objectives. This should not be so. Temporary setbacks should be seen as a resource that provides ideas from which one can learn. Remember that your setbacks are just a part of the process toward achieving your expectations and not a reason to quit the journey; rather, they provide an opportunity to evaluate and reassess for the next line of action on the playing field of life.

Let me illustrate with this a simple but relevant example. A young lady decides that she is going to shed some weight to fit into her wedding gown, but she becomes frustrated with her progress and quits. This has always been her line of action when faced with a temporary setback. This is very often the reason why most people never reach their fullest potential or achieve their goals. With so many unfulfilled dreams, they become frustrated in the process and quit before lasting results can be achieved.

Lack of Skills or Training: Denis Waitley said that "all of the top achievers I know are life-long learners looking for new skills, insights, and ideas. If they are not learning, they are not growing... not moving toward excellence." Sometimes, frustration comes from attempting a task that is beyond your training, experience, or expertise. This is common because our world is changing so rapidly. The way we are used to doing things is becoming obsolete. Most individuals in personal and professional environments are finding it daunting to stay abreast with the changing trends; this often results in frustration.

In our evolving world, skills that were relevant to a particular task yesterday could be obsolete today. These have brought untold frustration to many people. For example, the advent of the Internet has changed the way that we communicate and conduct business. We are faced with the challenge of attempting a task within a global environment that requires new skills, which often brings frustration to those involved. Jim Rohn remarked, "Formal education will make you a living; self-education will make you a fortune." The truth is that formal education will only get you so far, but consistent life-long learning will help you transform frustration, unlock the power to succeed, and give you a competitive advantage in any enterprise.

Lack of Details: Success is not in the accumulation of the details but the consistent and progressive action taken daily in harmony with little details possessed. Most people will agree that you must have all the details before you can take action and achieve meaningful results. However, as great as that may sound, I am convinced that this is not always the case. It is a known fact that struggling for details can cause anxiety, which ultimately leads to frustration.

Some individuals are not able to handle the fact that sometimes you can't wait to have all of the details before taking action. There are those who must have all of the details; otherwise, they cannot function and become frustrated. There are situations where you have to go ahead with what you have and get further details as you progress. Sometimes, individuals keep gathering details but never take any action. These individuals are said to have paralysis through analysis that is, spending too much time pondering unnecessary details.

Lack of Understanding: In any environment, frustration will occur when one does not understand what is being said. For example, I pastor a local church in Brussels, where we have a multinational congregation. During our service times, I preach in English with translations into French. I sometimes notice the frustration on the faces of some of the congregants, because they do not understand what I am saying. This could be quite disturbing to a lot of people; because you are not following the line of thought that is being developed, you cannot contribute appropriately and do not have a sense of belonging.

Have you been in situations where you were frustrated because you did not understand what has been said? This is a normal reaction, but it must not create dissension so much that it breaks down the line of communication. It will demotivate you and cause aggravation. This tends to happen because you are focusing on the feeling of frustration. You take the problem on yourself. It may be that the line of thought was not properly articulated. Again, in situations like this, one should begin to ask empowering questions.

Getting exasperated is not going to serve any meaningful purpose. Great relationships have been shattered because what was being said was not understood. Always remind yourself to understand others before you seek to be understood by others; this will help you see opportunities in the situation.

Memory Problems: We have all been guilty of this at some point. Examples include when you do not remember what you were supposed to do, your spouse's birthday, etc. All of these are the result of your inability to remember dates or events that are of great significance. This problem is countless, and it causes the people that have it to be frustrated and angry because they feel that they have ruined everyone's plans.

Loss: Loss of valuable information at work, time on something that is not rewarding, money in the stock market, or a great friendship can lead to frustration. Note that all of these losses in some form can minimize your chances of achieving your expectation. The level of frustration caused by loss differs depending on the interpretation of the situation. For instance, take the present state and condition of the world's economy. Most people are frustrated because of the losses that they have had to incur from this economic downturn.

Feeling Left Out: Feeling that you've been left out can result in frustration. For example, if you are working on a team where the input of every member is highly valued, but you did not have the opportunity to make your opinion known, this can lead to frustration. When this kind of emotional disposition builds up over some time, it can be devastating and result in low productivity, sarcasm, and indifference. No one enjoys being left out.

Fairness: A situation that has not been fairly handled can lead to frustration. For example, Mr. Desmond has worked diligently in a particular department and was due for a promotion. At the end of the year, he was not considered for the promotion. He feels that this is unfair and becomes frustrated with the company. These circumstances affect his attitude, which ultimately affects his productivity.

Lack of Definite Purpose: You are endowed with innate capabilities that are uniquely different and designed for a specific purpose. Most people do not understand this concept and consequently move from one endeavor to another in the hope of fulfilling one's purpose, only to end up frustrated. For instance, individuals can misinterpret their functional area and start their careers in a field in which they are weak or lack expertise. These individuals become frustrated because of the lack of results.

Lack of Money: It doesn't matter what you think about money. The truth of the matter is that lack of money has caused immeasurable frustration for many families across the nation. Too often, life doesn't turn out as expected. Money or the lack thereof plays a large role in one's ability to handle life's ups and downs. In Ecclesiastes 7:12, the preacher observed, "For wisdom is a defense, and money is a defense, but the excellency of knowledge is that wisdom giveth life to them that have it." Money is a defense; the lack of it makes you vulnerable to uncertain conditions. Many families are frustrated because they can't afford to educate their children or provide a basic standard of living.

This is not, by any means, an exhausting list of the root causes of frustration. However, the list here enumerated will serve as a guideline to demystify the numerous erroneous concepts that have been held over time. In the next chapter, we will now consider the *disadvantages of frustration.*

CHAPTER 3
DISADVANTAGES OF FRUSTRATION

"No matter how discouraged we get, God has not asked us to do the impossible."

George Grace

This book is about mastering and transforming frustrations into productive opportunities, producing outstanding results, and unlocking the power to succeed. However, it is imperative to understand some of the disadvantages of frustration. These disadvantages can be the outcome of short- or long-term frustration. This chapter presents a few common ones that are detrimental to your personal and professional fulfillment.

Frustration Kills your Dreams: One of the disadvantages of frustration is that it can stifle and kill your dreams if the necessary action is not taken to master and transform it. Some individuals give up completely. Dr. Martin Luther King, Jr. had a dream, but the fulfillment of that dream was not without frustration. The impact of frustration on the dreams and aspirations of a great number of people have left numerous dreams unfulfilled. Do not allow frustration to kill your dream, who was meant to be, and what you were meant to accomplish in your life.

Frustration Blinds Your Vision: In Proverbs 29:18a, we read: "Where there is no vision, the people perish." This implies that without vision, there is no direction. One translation of the Bible states that *where there is no vision people cast off restraint.* Another translation states that *where there is no vision, the people are uncontrolled.* With that said, it is possible to have a vision and not be fulfilled, because frustration has made your vision become a vague impression or a figment of your imagination that becomes impossible to accomplish. Do not let frustration blur your vision, for it takes vision to pursue your dream and reach your destination.

Frustration Destroys Relationships: Frustration is toxic to your relationships at work or home. You can destroy a significant relationship because you are frustrated over an event or situation. You might say some things that should not be said or act in ways you should not. This puts a strain on the relationship. For example, if you are frustrated with your spouse and utter words like "I made a mistake to have married you," this will draw some negative attention that will not be healthy for the relationship. This can also occur in the workplace with your colleagues. Do not let frustration abort your ordained relationship.

Frustration Robs You of Your Dignity: Dignity is your sense of pride and self-respect. Frustration will rob you of your sense of dignity if you respond negatively to it. You may have earned respect and admiration of family members or colleagues, but just for one incidence of frustration can rob you of your sense of pride. You'll never know who is watching. It could very well be someone with deep admiration for you. Do not allow frustration to rob you of your dignity; the price is often too great.

Frustration Destroys Self-confidence: Self-confidence is an attitude that allows individuals to have positive yet realistic views of themselves and their situations. It is one of the virtues that will take you to the next level in your personal and professional endeavors. This is simply confidence in yourself and your abilities. Frustration can intoxicate you so much that you will doubt yourself and your ability to do what you have to do to get the result that you are anticipating. Without self-confidence, you avoid taking risks due to the fear of failure, depending on the approval of others to feel good about yourself, and discount or ignore sincere compliments.

Frustration Increases Stress Levels: Stress is a mental, emotional, or physical strain caused by anxiety, overwork, or unmet expectations. Stress may cause such symptoms as high blood pressure or depression. By increasing your level of stress, frustration can affect your health considerably. The activities in which one is engaged are stressful enough. When you consider the cause of your stress, you will discover that it is not as bad as it seems. Hence, yielding to frustration will not help your stress level.

Frustration Destroys Morale: Morale is a state of individual psychological well-being based upon a sense of confidence, usefulness, and purpose. It is also the enthusiasm that an individual possesses at any particular time. This enthusiasm fuels and drives the motivation behind all his actions. Frustration is one of the emotional dispositions that affect the morale of an individual and causes it to deteriorate. Morale is the general level of confidence, self-esteem, or optimism felt by a person or group of people. Your morale will be destroyed if you ignore frustration. For instance, when one fails to accomplish objectives, this causes frustration, which will affect morale.

Frustration Fosters Negativity: This is one of the major disadvantages of frustration. Frustration fosters in an atmosphere where negativity prevails. When you dwell on it, the negative results overwhelm you. With a negative outcome, and this negativity will quickly spread the more that you complain about how disappointed you are with the outcome. This creates an atmosphere that is not conducive to creativity, growth, or productivity.

Frustration Distorts Your Outlook: Your outlook is the way that you perceive things to be. Your in-look determines your outlook; that is, the picture that you have inside of you dictates your outlook on life. Your outlook is a copy of the image that you have within; frustration distorts this image. Very often, your outlook is distorted by not looking at the circumstance from an objective perspective. For instance, you have a negative outlook on an event, person, or situation because of one single unpleasant occurrence.

Frustration Decreases Productivity: This emotional disposition decreases productivity in any instance. In the presence of frustration, you become uninspired, unmotivated, and disoriented in your thoughts, your attitude, and your actions, which ultimately affects your output. Productivity is not just what you have achieved but also how well you have used the resources at your disposal. The time spent whining about what should have been reduces the time spent on things that would move you in the direction of your desired goals.

Symptoms of Frustration

Your intent is not to focus on the symptoms of frustration but to discover the root cause. Therefore, to avoid these disadvantages, you must look out for symptoms to take immediate necessary action to transform frustration into creative opportunities and unlock the power to succeed. The following are common symptoms of frustrations:

» Fatigue

» Being overwhelmed

» Irritability

» Exhaustion (physical, mental, and emotional)

» Stress

» Lack of motivation

» Hopelessness

» Anger

» Doubt

One setback is dealing with symptoms without addressing the root cause of the problem. If this is the case, the same problem will surface again over and over again, which leads to frustration. Symptoms indicate that something is wrong and that you need to take action to remedy the situation. That said, once you are feeling any of these symptoms, apply the strategies in this book to negate the effects of frustration by transforming it into creative opportunities, and unlocking the power to succeed. We move on to the next chapter on *dealing with frustration*

CHAPTER 4

DEALING WITH FRUSTRATION

———————•⧫•———————

"All that is necessary to break the spell of inertia and frustration is to act as if it were impossible to fail."

Dorthea Brande

Asking Focused Questions

In everyday life, we are susceptible to frustration. Attempting to identify specifically what it is that you are frustrated about is critical to dealing with frustration. Frustration is often associated with problems or unmet expectations. In an attempt to translate frustration into productive opportunities and unlock the power to succeed, a series of focused and empowering questions should be asked.

It is interesting to note that questions can be empowering or disempowering. As a result, it is imperative that you put forth the right kinds of questions to become more focused, clear, creative, purposeful, and responsive. Questions can be used as tools to gather information and acquire knowledge about yourself, others, events, situations, and places. Answers to such questions are used to bring clarity and a better understanding of the situation.

"Quality questions create a quality life. Successful people ask better questions, and as a result, they get better answers," says Anthony Robbins. When frustration occurs, one of the ways of dealing with it is to ask a series of focused, empowering questions that will stimulate your thinking in a positive direction. These are questions that will make new facts, ideas, and principles useful, and important to you in the final analysis. For example:

- » How does this relate to what I already know?
- » What does this imply?
- » What other examples of this can I remember?
- » Why is this important to me (or others)?
- » Where else could this apply?
- » Where or how could I use this?
- » What does my plan of preparation entail?
- » How will I stay focused on results?
- » What is the measure of my effectiveness?

Most people have asked questions such as WHY has this happened to me. Such questions tend to undermine your abilities and sabotage your efforts; these types of questioning should be avoided by all means. To reiterate, the source of frustration could be internal and external. Appropriately identifying its source is important to help you formulate the right questions to be asked.

Questions That Transform Frustrations into Creative Opportunities and Unlock the Power to Succeed

Anthony Robbins observed, "The quality of one's life is directly related to the quality of questions one asks oneself." Here are some empowering questions that can improve the quality of your life, unlock the power to succeed, as well as help you transform frustration into a creative opportunity.

How Can I Make The Most Out of This Situation? This is a powerful question that will eliminate frustration every time. Here is what you need to do: Step back from the activity and take a look at the outcome of the situation rather than complaining about what is or is not. Ask yourself how you can make the most out of this situation. If you are held up in traffic that shows no sign letting up, think of how you can use your time. For instance, listen to uplifting audiobooks or meditate. While the traffic is at a standstill, journal about something you are passionate about or begin writing the outlines of your soon to be released book. This will help you make the most use of the situation instead of yielding to frustration, which can ruin your whole day.

What Is The Perfect Outcome? This question can be applied to any area of your life, either personal or professional. When you have feelings of frustration because of an unfulfilled expectation or an uncomfortable relationship with a loved one, you should ask yourself what the perfect outcome would be. You may have lost sight of the ideal outcome because of the events that have transpired in your life. This question redirects and reaffirms your focus to help you move in the right direction, focusing on the root cause rather than the negative outcome. This line of questioning empowers you and motivates strategic action.

What Exactly Am I Trying to Achieve? There are moments in the events of your life when there seems to be confusion as to what your real objective is. No matter how hard you try, you are continually met with unforeseen crises. When faced with these kinds of challenges, most individuals do not know what to do, and this is frustrating. Sometimes frustration renders your objectives and goals vague; in moments like these, you need to step aside and ask yourself the question of what you are trying to achieve. Again, this will help you to keep perspective rather than allowing your frustration to disorient and make you less motivated from achieving your desired outcome.

What Actions Have I Taken To Lead Me To These Results? Results are always products of action or inaction. Consequently, when the result that you are producing is frustration, some actions or inactions must have led to such a result. One of the reasons that you are producing the kinds of results that you have right now is your course of action or inaction. Hence, empowering questions such as what actions you have taken that led to the outcome is invaluable. As you recognize these actions or inactions that are producing these unwanted results, you now can correct them to produce the desired results.

Are There an Alternative Means To Achieve My Anticipated Outcome? Again, this could be in a personal or professional situation. Let us consider a work scenario. Suppose that your boss left you with a project to complete within the next two days. You faithfully work on this project only to discover that you have not arrived at the anticipated conclusion, and time is no longer on your side. This made you upset, stressed, and frustrated. You decide to quit and return the unfinished project to your boss without seeking other ways of solving the problem.

This is the appropriate moment to ask if there are alternative ways to achieve your anticipated outcome.

What is My Self-talk? Self-talk is what you are saying to yourself. It is your inner dialogue. Positive self-talk is most needed when you are going through a challenge. Studies have shown that your self-talk determines 95% of your emotions. Ask what you are saying to yourself that is causing my frustration. This is an important question because words are very powerful; they can set the tone for how you respond to a situation, which will ultimately create a positive or negative outcome. Therefore, if you are having a feeling of frustration, the foremost question to ask is how you are interpreting the situation. A great way to transform frustration into creative opportunities and unlock the power to succeed is to use positive affirmation in your self-talk.

What Valuable Lesson is This Situation Teaching Me? I believe that every situation can teach you valuable lessons. There are two consistent opportunities that any situation affords you: the opportunity to contribute positively and the opportunity to learn something valuable. When you are feeling frustrated, ask what valuable lesson the situation is teaching you. This will help you look at the situation from a positive perspective, develop ideas, and gather the information that will be critical to your next line of action.

What Past Conditioning and Old Beliefs Stand in My Way? Everyone that I have worked with has past experiences or beliefs that stand in the way of significant progress. The next question is important because you have past conditioning or old beliefs that are mitigating your progress and are responsible for your frustration. Identifying beliefs that no longer serve your purpose is vital to transforming frustrations into creative opportunities and unlocking the power to succeed. This will help you gain perspective on the issues that are responsible for your frustration.

Are My Expectations S.M.A.R.T? We all have expectations. Many people become frustrated when their expectations are not met. Ask if those expectations were SMART: specific, measurable, attainable, realistic, and time-oriented. For example, suppose that you are starting your own business and plan to make a million dollars in the first year. As much as this is a worthwhile goal, it's unrealistic. This would not be a S.M.A.R.T expectation.

What Is and Isn't Working? Asking these questions helps you to evaluate your action plan. Remember the old saying, "Back to the drawing board!" Do not hesitate to revisit your projects whenever your plans are not working. Frustration is a powerful energy that can be productive or destructive. Rather than allowing the destructive energy of frustration to cripple you, translate that energy into something productive by reassessing all of the working components, such as your goals, action plans, and expectations. Make the necessary changes to create new results.

What Purpose Does It Serve? There is a purpose to everything in life. How the events of your life turn out in the final analysis ultimately depends on your response to the situation. When frustration occurs, ask what purpose it serves. This kind of question will give you the proper perspective. Dr. Myles Munroe states that "when the purpose of a thing is not known abuse is inevitable." Knowing the purpose that frustration is meant to serve will enhance your learning abilities and in turn, increase your productivity.

What is The Bright Side in All of This? With so much happening around us, there seems to be no room for even considering the light at the end of the tunnel. When an event doesn't turn out in the manner anticipated, ask yourself what the bright side is. This is an empowering question that will produce answers and move you in a positive direction. This kind of question enables you to see something positive and to make the changes that are necessary to bring about the anticipated expectation.

Is This Feedback? When you consider your frustration as feedback, you will tend to respond positively. This feedback could mean that something is not working right or that the proper course of action has not been taken. For instance, if you want to discuss with your spouse and he or she indicates a lack of interest, see that response of lack of interest as positive feedback. This then enables you to understand what is working and what is not working. It will also help you to scrutinize your goals and expectations. Your ability to accept this reaction as feedback and make corrections to your line of action is vital for turning your frustration into productive opportunity.

Am I Comfortable with What I'm Doing? There are always easy, effortless ways and the right way of doing things. Many people get frustrated in moments when they are engaged in certain activities. When this emotional disposition prevails, ask if you are comfortable with what you are doing. You do not have to be a genius to respond to that question. If you respond candidly, you will break the circle of what is frustrating you and empower yourself to decide what you are comfortable doing.

Have I Done Enough for Myself? Experts in the field of personal and professional development argue that "you can improve on anything by at least 10%." Have you, or is there something more you can do or improve on? You can improve your skills in any aspect of life. To be discontent can be dangerous, but in small amounts, it allows you to do incredible things.

If I Took My Current Task Just One Step Further, What Else Could I Achieve? You never know what is on the horizon. In moments of frustration, ask what you could achieve if you took just one step further. You will be amazed at the number of endorphins that will be secreted into your system and the response that your conscious mind will produce in response to that question. This will make you see possibilities even in the face of difficulties.

What is My Motivation? What motivates you? Honesty is of great consequence in identifying and responding to this query. It is your responsibility to discover what motivates you. There are so many things that can make people happy; to choose may be the hardest part. When frustration sets in, you should look at what your motivation is. This will keep you moving in the right direction rather than giving up on your dream.

What Makes You Tick? So, what is it that makes you function? What is it that brings the best out in you? You can become just about anything you want, but attaining your expectations may seem difficult and cause you to give up before you even start the journey. For any given task, you must determine what makes you function to the best of your ability. Always remember that self-improvement is not just about the physical or philosophical change—it's a process that permeates every aspect of human nature.

CHAPTER 5

THOMAS EDISON & COLONEL SANDERS

"When a man really desires a thing so deeply that he is willing to stake his entire future on a single turn of the wheel in order to get it, he is sure to win."

Thomas Edison

Thomas Edison was expelled from school in the sixth grade. His parents were told that it would be a waste of time to spend money educating him because he was not particularly capable of anything great. Of course, Edison went on to become one of the greatest inventors of the modern age. Edison failed a thousand times before he invented the light bulb. This failure would have discouraged most people. Imagine the amount of frustration. What allowed Edison to continue?

A Desire to Learn: Edison had a desire to learn from his mistakes. As we encounter failures, frustration is inevitable, but we must focus on a higher purpose. The desire to learn what is working and what is not will ultimately bring our desired outcome to fruition.

A Desire to Do the Impossible: Edison had a desire to do the impossible. Somehow, embedded within his soul, he knew that what seemed impossible was possible. Extraordinary achievers like Donald Trump, Robert Kiyosaki, Tim Darnell, and Mathew Ashimolowo all possess this trait. They confronted failure but kept moving in spite of the momentary impediment. They conquered their frustration no matter the challenges that they confronted in their process.

Love of A Challenge: Obstacles are what we see when we take our eyes off the goal. Edison loved the challenge. You have to love the challenges that you face as you pursue your dreams. The idea of been repulsed by the challenge is one of the major causes of frustration. In other, for Edison to succeed, he had to consider each failure as a challenge to try harder, look deeper, and focus on the final destination.

Resilience: Charlie "Tremendous" Jones said, "It is not how hard you fall, but how high you bounce back that counts." Edison may have failed countless times, but he kept bouncing back. You must not allow frustrations to destroy your resilience.

Willingness to Accept Disappointment: Some individuals complain about their disappointments until they become incarcerated by frustration. Be willing to accept disappointment. A willingness to accept disappointments is not weakness, but of strength in that, you will not accept your disappointments as final but with a readiness to seek ways to turn your disappointments into appointments.

Unshakable Perseverance: Edison *had* to stay the course. Can you imagine what his friends would have said to him or how they ridiculed him? I think that he must have become a laughing stock of his contemporaries, but none of this deterred him from his goals and objectives. There will be times when your goal seems very bleak; this will breed frustration. It takes unshakeable perseverance to meet your expectations.

The Right Perspective: Edison had the right perspective of things. To have failed a thousand times meant discovering more opportunities. Attitude is everything. The right perspective will solidify your courage even amid difficult and frustrating times.

Power of Focus: Edison once wrote, "My success is due more to my ability to work continuously on one thing without stopping than to any other single quality." He knew that his failure was a temporary setback. He focused on the result and continued to work. Edison used frustration as a stepping stone to fulfilling his goal.

It is imperative to note that frustration is common to us all, from the church house to the White House. It is what you become in the face of what you go through that will determine whether you succeed or fail. Therefore, in times of frustration, your attitude should be that this event will eventually pass. Remember, this should always be your attitude. Don't give in, and don't give up.

Colonel Sanders at 65

At the age of 65, Colonel Sanders began with a simple chicken recipe spent two years driving across the United States, looking for restaurants to buy his chicken recipe. He was turned down 1009 times before he got a positive response. The rest is history: Sanders went on to create a business empire known as Kentucky Fried Chicken. He was frustrated but refused to allow frustration to end his dream.

Stories like these can be found throughout history. They provide great examples of people who turned frustration into opportunity. The next chapter discusses *growing through frustration*

CHAPTER 6

GROWING THROUGH FRUSTRATION

"Everything is a gift of the universe, every joy, anger, jealousy, frustration, or separateness. Everything is perfect either for our growth or our enjoyment."

Ken Keyes, Jr.

"It is not what happens to a man, but what he does after it has happened that counts in a man's life." Richard Onebamoi. You may not be able to stop frustration from occurring, but you can determine the direction in which you will go. In the same light, you cannot stop thoughts from entering your mind, but you can stop disempowering thoughts from taking residence.

It is not the individual that does everything possible to avoid or endure frustrations but the individual that uses frustration as an advantage that becomes an extraordinary achiever. No one is immune to frustration. These things are a part of life. Frustration can make or break you depending on our choices.

"Maturity is the ability to think, speak, and act out your feelings within the bounds of dignity. The measure of your maturity is how spiritual you become amid your frustrations" (unknown source). There is the notion that you mature as you age, but this is not always the case. You must make a deliberate decision to grow. Most people have failed to realize that frustration is a means whereby you can be built up if you properly harness the issues that are responsible for this emotional discomfort.

According to the Bible, there is nothing that has happened to any man that is new under the earth. Someone else must have gone through what you are going through at this moment. Your frustration is not something new. Instead of playing the victim, play the victor. You are just a decision away from turning that frustrating event into encouragement.

Strategies for Overcoming Frustration

Pete Zafra stated, "Yesterday's failures are today's seeds that must be diligently planted to be able to abundantly harvest tomorrow's success." It is important to understand that yesterday's failures are just events that occurred in the pursuit of your expectations. Therefore, in dealing with frustration, you must consider yesterday's failures as seeds with endless positive possibilities that must be planted in the soil of today, which will yield outstanding results tomorrow. With that said, let us examine some simple but profound strategies for transforming frustration into creative opportunities.

Seek God's Help: Phillip Keller remarked, "God's will carries within it all that has been set in motion for our welfare and benefit. He has our best interest at heart." You might have heard this in the past, but have you tried asking God for help? Praying and talking to God about your problem can be very effective. Although the answers might not come to you right away, you cannot go wrong by relying on God for assistance. You never know how God will work in your life. All you can do is to do your best each day, hope and believe for the best, and take it in stride with God's help. God will help you through your problems if you ask.

Quiet Time: Develop a habit of having quiet times. These are moments when you step aside from all your activities as you begin to feel overwhelmed or frustrated. Jesus often went to solitary places to be alone. Bishop David Oyedope has a quiet place called his thinking room. Your solitary place is a place of rest where you can brainstorm and strategize. A place like this is a must-have. These are quality times that you can rejuvenate and put things into perspective. The importance of quiet time cannot be overemphasized, and its benefits are unparalleled.

Benefits of Quiet Times:

Here are just a few benefits, why having quiet time is important and the need to integrate into your daily routine:

- » You can focus better
- » Your thoughts and ideas are refined
- » You have clarity of mind
- » You are relaxed and feel rejuvenated
- » You can strategize

» You can bring harmony to the spirit, mind, and body.

» You can understand and see clearly what you could not see before.

"I Will" Power: Eddie Robinson stated "The will to win, the desire to succeed, the urge to reach your potential… these are the keys that will unlock the door to personal excellence." When you are confronted with seemingly impossible goals, the "I will" power transform your frustration into creative opportunities and unlocks the door to success. It is this power that will keep you focused on the objectives, strengthen your belief that it is possible, and garner the faith to continue in spite of the odds.

Identify Root Cause(s) of Frustration: The law of cause and effect teaches that for every action, there is an equal reaction. For every effect in your life, there is a cause. You can use this law to your benefit if you understand what actions produce positive results in your personal or professional life. Consider frustration as an effect with a cause and identify its root cause(s). For example, there are many reasons why your car may not start, such as faulty ignition, dead battery, or lack of fuel. Identifying these causes can solve your problem, which then eliminates your frustration.

Confront Frustration: Our frustration tends to paralyze us, holding us back from taking constructive action in the direction of our definite purpose. There are those who avoid the situation entirely. The problem with this line of action is the fact that you miss out on valuable lessons you would have learned from addressing the issue. From my experience, this becomes a vicious circle. You are unable to deal with similar situations positively because you did not confront the issue the first time.

Examine The Situation Responsible For Frustration: Examine every situation for valuable lessons. You will avoid a lot of pain if you take the time to examine the situation responsible for your frustration before you make conclusions.

Use a Valuable Learning Tool: See the situation as a learning experience. With a positive attitude, belief in yourself, and faith in God, you will find yourself in a better situation and frame of mind. Instead of complaining and making yourself miserable, ask how you can use frustration as a valuable learning tool. Looking closely, there are always valuable lessons to be learned that will better prepare you down the road when another situation like it arises. With the experiences that you have gained, you will be in a better position to make decisions that will make you more productive in the direction of your objectives.

Seek Counsel: Seek counsel for unresolved questions in your heart. Proverbs 15:22 states that "without counsel, purposes are disappointed: but in the multitude of counselors they are established." The people with the most resolved questions are those that take advantage of the wisdom and grow from the wealth of knowledge provided by counselors, mentors, or coaches. The value of having mentors in one's life cannot be stressed enough. Not only can they multiply your effectiveness, but they can also act as guidance counselors to help you remain focused and, in some cases, out of trouble.

Define The Object of Frustration As A Goal: Take a minute or two actually to define the problem. Once you have identified the object of frustration, that is, what is responsible for your frustration, you should view that challenge as a goal to be achieved. For instance, it could be your lack of skills that result in ineffectiveness. You can set the goal of acquiring new skills. It is often more effective to ensure that you understand the problem, its symptoms, and its causes before proceeding.

Obtain Information On How To Solve The Problem: This requires an in-depth study of how to resolve the problems that bring about frustration. You must also identify the level of competence of those who can provide suggestions for the solution of the problem. Weigh the potential benefits and costs of all possible options, considering the time that it will take and the resources that will be involved.

Eliminate The Obvious: What I mean by the obvious is anything that serves as a positive catalyst for the attainment of your objectives. This is a strategy that I have used in helping individuals who are frustrated and do not know how to begin dealing with challenges. I begin by asking them to eliminate what is obvious to them, such as things or activities that move them in the direction of their anticipated expectations. Then, I ask them now to put the other things that seem to serve their purpose or goals negatively into proper perspective and deal with them accordingly.

Do Not Precipitate Actions: James 1:19b says, "Wherefore, my beloved brethren, let every man be swift to hear, slow to speak, slow to wrath." This implies that you perceive the lessons behind the frustration. Be slow to speak and slow to anger; in other words, do not precipitate your actions. In retrospect, gather the entire puzzle together, take a peek into the big picture, and make sure you have done your homework thoroughly before pursuing any line of action.

New Possibilities: Take every difficult situation, as a new possibility rather than a problem. Every adverse situation that occurs can become an opportunity to grow, to be creative, to become a better person, and to achieve much more in the process. This will broaden your horizons, increase your learning ability, and expand your ability to become a resource because of what you have become in the process of taking action.

Change Your Focus: Focus on what you CAN do, not what you CAN'T do. Think positive thoughts (*Yes, I can do this!*). In other words, you must change your focus from the negative to the positive to align with your core values, moving in the direction of your anticipated goal. It is true that we tend to gravitate towards that which captivates our focus. We become what we focus on. Hence, when we are experiencing frustration, we must instantly change and realign our focus on the elements that will help us produce a different outcome. Do not forget that ***whatever captures your focus controls your life.***

Become Solution-oriented: You must be solution-oriented to deal with frustration. Your mind must stay alert to new ideas and be willing to adapt to changes. Seek out solutions that will solve problems, and learn to empower yourself with questions that will serve as a catalyst and not hinder you from taking action. Discover where the difficulty lies and seek ways to solve it. Better yet, ask for help from someone you trust. This will help you to deal with the frustration that occurs.

Visualize A Positive Outcome: Allow yourself to visualize the anticipated outcomes or benefits of the goals that you have set. Hebrews 12:2b states that "who for the joy that was set before him endured the cross, despising the shame, and is set down at the right hand of the throne of God." In other words, Jesus did not look at the present circumstance, which was frustrating by all account as his final reality; rather, he set his focus on the reward of the price paid to achieve the goal, which was our redemption. To frustration-proof your life, you must focus on positive outcomes.

Seek To Understand: Whether it is a person or a group of people who are responsible for your frustration, always seek to understand before you are understood. Ask questions to make sure that others understand what has been discussed, and get their feedback so that there will be no surprises. Understand that frustration is common to everyone and that you are not alone. What sets you apart from others is the way that you respond to emotions when they occur. Take a profound look at what is making you frustrated to see if there are ways that you are contributing to it, and then take action to remedy the problem.

Be Enthusiastic: Henry Ford stated, "Enthusiasm is the yeast that makes your hopes shine to the stars. Enthusiasm is the sparkle in your eyes, the swing in your gait. The grip of your hand, the irresistible surge of will and energy to execute your ideas." One of the things that frustration does is to stifle your enthusiasm. However, if your enthusiasm stays afloat amid your challenges, that irresistible surge of will and energy will execute your ideas and transform whatever handicaps you into opportunities.

Never Consider The Possibility of Failure: You have to see every failure as a postponed success. Look at every setback as a new opportunity to transform frustration into productivity. Thomas J. Watson, the founder of IBM, said that "to become more successful, you must double your failure rate because then you will learn from those failures." Look for the good in every frustrating situation and do your best to benefit from it. Napoleon Hill once wrote that "every difficulty contains the seed of an equal or greater blessing."

Overcome Negative Self-talk and Self-sabotage: It is often easy to talk down to yourself and indulge in activities that will sabotage your efforts when you are not achieving your expectations. You must overcome the tendency of negative self-talk by choosing to include positive affirmation in your life and by avoiding self-sabotaging endeavors that do not move you toward your anticipated outcome. Jim Rohn said, "Positive affirmation without discipline is delusion." Discipline is a core component in overcoming negative self-talk and self-sabotage.

Take Action: Make a definite commitment from the start that when you see a NEGATIVE input, you will take immediate action to turn it into a POSITIVE input. This is where you as a hard-working, sincere, and loving person take the unnecessary beating at the hand of frustration because you allow this negative input to sabotage your performance by not doing something about it. These negative and toxic inputs, such as stress, doubt, and fuzzy expectations, can undermine your performance, resulting in frustration. Hence, it's imperative to take action to turn them into opportunities that will produce a positive performance. Let's now move to the subject *fear factor.*

CHAPTER 7

FEAR FACTOR

"You can conquer almost any fear if you will only make up your mind to do so. For remember, fear doesn't exist anywhere except in the mind."

Dale Carnegie

How to Deal With the Fear Factor of Frustration

First and foremost in dealing with the fear factor of frustration, it must be understood that fear in itself is part of the human condition. It is healthy until it becomes something that can incarcerate you when the appropriate measure is not taken. Quite obviously, fear is everywhere. People are fearful about job security, income, shelter, and so forth.

Franklin D. Roosevelt remarked, "The only thing we have to fear is fear itself." It is important to understand this aspect of human nature because fear tends to dominate and distort your consciousness. For instance, the fear of the government can torment you when your tax returns are due; this fear of government ought to serve as a signal to get your taxes done. Instead of taking action to rectify the situation, you submit to fear.

Most people allow fear to immobilize them. Marianne Williamson wrote: "Our deepest fear is not that we are inadequate. Our deepest fear is that we are powerful beyond measure. It is our light, not our darkness that most frightens us. We ask ourselves, 'Who am I to be brilliant, gorgeous, talented, and fabulous?' Actually, who are you not to be? You are a child of God. Your playing small does not serve the world. There is nothing enlightened about shrinking so that other people won't feel insecure around you. We are all meant to shine, as children do. We were born to make manifest the glory of God that is within us. It's not just in some of us; it's in everyone. And as we let our light shine, we unconsciously permit other people to do the same. As we are liberated from our fear, our presence automatically liberates others".

As you move forward on your journey from where you are to where you want to be in pursuit of your purpose, you are going to have to confront some of your fears. Marianne Williamson emphasized that "our deepest fear is not that we are inadequate. Our deepest fear is that we are powerful beyond measure." Whenever you start a new project, embark on a new undertaking, or put yourself out there, there's usually *some* fear involved. Unfortunately, most people let fear stop them from taking the necessary steps to achieve their dreams.

The acronym FEAR is often referred to as False Expectations Appearing Real or False Evidence Appearing Real or Forget Everything And Reload. A lot of people are driven by fear of things that aren't real but appear to be real. Their fears may be a result of a distressing experience, unrealistic expectations, and trouble in their formative years, or even uncertainty.

Notwithstanding the cause, fear-driven people often miss great opportunities in life, because they are terrified to undertake any project or responsibility. As an alternative, they play it safe, avoid risks, and try to maintain the status quo by all means. Fear is a self-imposed prison that will keep you from becoming what God intends for you to be.

You must move against it with the weapons of faith and courage. Where fear is found, frustration is creeping around. Once fear is banished, you will be able to transform frustration into creative opportunity and unlock the power to succeed.

From what we see and understand, your fears can incarcerate and immobilize you in your life. It also can kill your creative abilities and the power of imagination, if efforts are not made to overcome it. However, research has shown that some fears are healthy. In other words, fear is a way of signaling that you might be approaching a dangerous situation or something is not working accurately; you need to take action in resolving or remedy the situation. One of the solutions is to take action to dismantle and overcome fear. Next, we will examine some common fears.

Fear of Change: Fear of change refers to false evidence of change appearing real, which often results in frustration. Most people want to maintain the status quo since the change of any kind threatens the present modus operandi. To overcome fear and turn it into a productive opportunity, we must look for those factors that predispose us toward fear. We all know that change is not easy, that it can be threatening, and that it can cause uneasiness. However, change also presents opportunities that won't be there if we keep doing things the way that we have done them.

Most people dread change to the extent that the thought of change causes frustration. This is so because we have become so comfortable with our present status quo that changing seems like an impossible task. Dorothy Thompson reveals, "The most destructive element in the human mind is fear. Fear creates aggressiveness." Your fear can paralyze you, holding you back from taking constructive action that is congruent with your dreams and goals.

Fear of Criticism: This is a major setback for the majority of people. I must say that criticism is healthy, depending on your response to it. It is astonishing what our minds go through when we are criticized. You may get frustrated, fearful, or angry with the person or persons who are criticizing. We often avoid certain activities due to fear of criticism. Criticism is merely an opinion, not who you are. This is how you should look at criticism: as someone else's opinion. Some individuals can't handle criticism without becoming frustrated. You can decide to use criticism as positive leverage, or allow it to disempower you.

Fear of Failure: The fear of failure is, by far, the most common fear faced by potential achievers. For some reason, we are afraid to fail. The fear of failure is perhaps the strongest force holding people back from reaching their potential. It prevents them from stepping out of their comfort zone, trying new things, or even daring to fulfill their dreams. Of course, this is very frustrating and disappointing. When you anticipate that you will fail, it is the fear of failure that hurts far more than the failure itself.

Thomas Edison stated, "To double your success rate, you need to first double your failures." He said, "I didn't fail 1000 times. I just found 1000 ways not to make a light bulb." Failure is the pathway to success. Fall in love with mistakes; they are learning experiences. Success phraseology serves you for success; failure phraseology serves you for failure, which is why you must change your language. Exercise every night before bed; enumerate at least ten successes of the day. Consequently, to transform frustration into creative opportunity and unlock the power to succeed, you must address the issue of fear of failure.

Fear of Rejection: Fear of rejection has immobilized most people in every area of life. You refuse to get out there to do what you know you should be doing for fear of rejection. For example, a salesperson hesitates to ask for a sale because he is afraid of being rejected just as an employee might refuse to ask for a raise for fear that his request will be rejected. The fear of rejection permeates your personal or professional life and prevents you from taking action that will move you in the direction of your anticipated expectation.

Fear of the Unknown: The unknown is a major source of fear. It is the fear of not being sure what will happen. When you do not know exactly what you are dealing with or what to expect from the circumstance, the potential consequences will be overblown. We tend to have drawbacks; as a result, the unknown is not comfortable, and breeds fear. In a territory with which you are unfamiliar, fear always creeps in and hinders your ability to make decisions.

Being Overly Cautious: This is a form of fear that indicates that you should be careful. It is the tendency to look at everything from a negative standpoint instead of concentrating on the means to succeed.

Waiting for the "right time" that never seems to come is indicative of being overly cautious, which in most cases, is because of fear; this eventually leads to frustration. Look at the desired reality instead of the present reality.

Procrastination: Procrastination refers to putting off until tomorrow what should have been done today. You refuse to accept responsibility; are willing to compromise rather than fight for what you know is right, and bargain with life for a penny instead of harnessing the riches. Procrastination is an enemy of progress. It will sabotage your plans and cause you a lot of frustrations.

How to Overcome the Fear Factor of Frustration

Confront Your Fears: One of the best ways to deal with the fear factor is to confront your fears. It is to your disadvantage to shy away from your fear, because it will linger on. You see, what you do no confront today will live on to torment you tomorrow. Learning to challenge your fears will help you discover the resilience within that you thought you did not possess. It will also help you to discover what fear is all about.

Feed Your Mind and Spirit: Feed on positive and uplifting materials to banish fear from your life. Just as you feed your body with natural food to gain nutrients, your mind and spirit also need to be fed to function. Treat your mind and spirit to the best mental and spiritual nutrition that is available, for it's all you've got. Set aside time to read or listen to informative audiobooks, for this is invaluable.

Have a Proper Perspective: Many people are tormented by fear and frustrated with life as a result. One reason is having the wrong view of the situation. When events causing fear in your life are put into perspective, they will become false evidence appearing real. Once you understand what fear is and take congruent action in the direction of your anticipated expectation, fear will dissipate into the atmosphere.

Divide the Task into Smaller Segments: When facing a current or upcoming task that overwhelms you with fear and anxiety, prioritize the task into a series of smaller tasks and then complete one at a time. Completing these smaller tasks will make stress more manageable and increase your chances of success. Lao Tzu observed, "The journey of a thousand miles begins with a step."

Get Help: The ability to leverage help from others is invaluable in dealing with fear. Enlist the help of others as fear creeps into your life. This can come in the form of prayers, encouragement, insight, mentoring, and counseling. Very often, it is quite helpful to know that someone is standing with you in challenging times; hence, it is important always to seek the help of others as you seek solutions to your fears.

Do Not Exaggerate: Sometimes, we tend to blow a situation out of proportion, which causes tremendous fear because it distorts the facts. In my work, I have always told people that a situation exaggerated is a platform for breeding fear that will produce anxiety and frustration in the final analysis.

Take Action: The best way to reduce fear and build self-confidence is by taking action. Whenever fear arises, take action immediately to address it; do not wait until it deteriorates beyond what you can now deal with. Ambrose Redmoon remarked, "Courage is not the absence of fear, but rather the judgment that something else is more important than fear." Courage is uncommon in times of fear; possess it to take action in dealing with fear.

It is imperative to understand that both faith and fear will always sail into the harbor of your mind, but only faith should be allowed to anchor. Fear must be banished from the shores of your mind because you need that space for something more productive that will move you in the direction of your dreams. Next, we will examine *burnout syndrome.*

CHAPTER 8

THE BURNOUT SYNDROME

Our fatigue is often caused not by work, but by worry, frustration, and resentment.

Dale Carnegie

Burnout Defined

Merriam Webster Dictionary defines burnout as "exhaustion of physical or emotional strength or motivation usually as a result of prolonged stress or frustration." Burnout is a state of being extremely tired or ill, either physically or mentally, because you have worked too hard. It is the psychological exhaustion and diminished efficiency resulting from working too hard or prolonged exposure to stress. It is the exhaustion that results from excessive demands, which may be self-imposed or externally imposed by family, friends, work, or society. These demands deplete one's energy, coping mechanisms, and internal resources. When you are burned out, problems seem insurmountable, and everything looks bleak.

Burnout can be compared to a rocket that has used all of its fuel. When all of the elements that are necessary to provide the strength, motivation, and aptitude to carry out activities are used up, this results in burnout. This could easily lead to frustration because your productivity will drop dramatically.

How Do I Deal with Burnout?

If constant stress has you feeling physically, mentally, and emotionally exhausted, you may be suffering from burnout. You have to keep the important things important. It is imperative to note that technology is developing at an astronomical pace. We have not realized that the things that were meant for our pleasure have become the source of our exhaustion. We must learn to create pleasure out of whatever we do.

You are burned out because you have worked too hard or have used up your fuel, which resulted in physical or mental fatigue. You no longer have the energy to work with others. The solution is to keep the important things important. Prioritize your tasks. Set realistic and attainable goals. Learn how to delegate or ask for help.

Burnout Symptoms

The symptoms of burnout can vary from individual to individual, and from situation to situation, hence it is imperative that we do not evaluate this situation by just single metrics, but the following are some warning signs that indicate burnout:

- » Powerlessness
- » Hopelessness

» Emotional Exhaustion

» Detachment

» Isolation

» Irritability

» Feelings of Depression and Isolation

» Physical Fatigue

» Feeling Trapped

» Failure

» Despair

» Cynicism

» Apathy

» Lack of Desire

» Decreased Productivity

» Increased Absence and Tardiness

» Abuse of Alcohol/Drugs

» Boredom

» Feelings of Anger and Resentment

» Sleep Problems

» Inability to Relax

» Disillusionment

» Feelings of Helplessness

» Frustration

» Lack of Power to Change Events

The first step to getting help is acknowledging that you need help. The second step is to seek professional guidance. The road to finding your perfect work can be challenging, but it is also empowering and life-changing.

What are Some Factors Leading to Burnout?

On close examination, it has been purported that there are both external and internal factors contributing to burnout. Let us now examine these factors:

External Factors: These are the external drivers that are responsible for burnout personally and professionally.

- » A stressful and disorganized environment
- » Stressful, anxious, tense, or hostile people
- » The focus of control is outside of yourself and in the hands of others
- » Inability to control others outside of yourself
- » Lack of preparation for the task

Internal Factors: These are the inner drivers that are contributing to personal or professional burnout.

- » Motivation to do your best all of the time
- » A reaction to a specific negative or stressful stimulus
- » Mourning for the self-image of "being special."
- » Distorted thinking
- » Depression over not being good enough
- » Not being able to meet an idealistic vision of self as a competent worker or family member

Burnout Chart

Here is a simplified Burnout Chart. Use it whenever you start to wonder if you are working too hard. Compare notes with your spouse or colleagues when using this chart. Occasionally, you may wish to rate each other; you may also wish for your friends to rate you. Your grown children would also be good to consult occasionally regarding what is on this chart.

Effective burnout-busting strategies include taking care of yourself emotionally and physically, asking for help when you need it, and staying connected to other people. When you discover that you are suffering from burnout, shut down, get away, and take a break; relaxation, vacation, and exercise are the best medicine.

Rating Scale:

Never – 0; Sometimes – 1; Often – 2; Usually – 3; Always - 4.

_____1.   I'm tired.

_____2.   I'm depressed.

_____3.   I'm physically exhausted.

_____4.   I'm emotionally exhausted.

_____5.   I feel wiped out.

_____6   I feel burned out.

_____7.   I'm unhappy.

_____8.   I'm rundown.

_____9. I feel trapped.

_____10. I feel worthless.

_____11. I'm weary.

_____12. I'm troubled.

_____13 I'm disillusioned and resentful.

_____14. I feel weak.

_____15. I feel things are hopeless.

_____16. I feel rejected.

_____17. I'm anxious.

If your total is more than 20, then it's time to get concerned. Above 30 points gives cause for alarm, and more than 40 points mean that you are burning out. Professional consultation is in order.

Understanding How to Overcome Stress

"If you are distressed by anything external, the pain is not due to the thing itself, but to your estimation of it; and this you have the power to revoke at any moment." Marcus Aurelius Antoninus. Stress can be one single factor that causes a person to become unproductive personally or professionally, hence it crucial that you know how to by all means.

Stress Defined: Dorland's Medical Dictionary for Health Consumers defines stress as "a state of physiological or psychological strain caused by adverse stimuli that tend to disturb the functioning of an organism."

Understanding how to overcome stress is imperative because studies have shown that 80% to 90% of all diseases are stress-related. I suppose that these figures are staggering enough to make the subject of stress a priority in our lives. A lot of people are stressed today for numerous reasons.

Causes of Stress: Stress is caused by many different factors. Identifying its origin is invaluable in providing solutions. Here is a list of the causes of stress:

» Events that are considered a threat to one's general wellbeing

» Changes in one's physical or social environment

» Fear of failure

» Fear of losing one's job

» Fear of rejection

» Financial challenges

» Problems with family members

Remedies

Whenever you are feeling stressed, you need to take action to change the state or condition. The following suggestions will help overcome stress:

» Take a break from whatever you are doing.

» Get away from the problem for a while.

» Take a deep breath.

» Reassess and describe the source of stress.

» Change your focus.

» Come to terms with the fact that there are some things beyond your control.

» If stress is beginning to affect your health, seek professional help.

» Having quiet moments.

Stress is related to frustration. You have to pay close attention to both internal and external stressors. Most of the things that you are stressed about will not necessarily turn out the way that you fear it might. By understanding this, you will be empowered to overcome stress and transform frustration into creative opportunities and the power to succeed.

How to Deal with Depression

Many people are susceptible to depression. This illness can be triggered by stress or frustrating circumstances in one's life. At this point, you may not have experienced depression, but perhaps you probably have met someone who has.

According to the Gale Encyclopaedia of Medicine, depression is "a state of being depressed marked especially by sadness, inactivity, difficulty with thinking and concentration, a significant increase or decrease in appetite and time spent sleeping, feelings of dejection and hopelessness, and sometimes suicidal thoughts or an attempt to commit suicide. It represents extreme low moods that last a long time and makes a person feel sad, irritable, or empty. Depression is said to occur because of a chemical imbalance in the brain. It could also occur due to the changes in one's personal or professional life."

Types of Depression

Clinical Depression: This is a mental disorder characterized by a pervasive low mood, loss of interest in a person's usual activities, and diminished ability to experience a pleasure.

Dysthymia: This is a mood disorder that falls within the depression spectrum. It is often considered chronic depression, but with less severity than major depression. This disorder tends to be a chronic, long-lasting illness.

Bipolar Depression: This is where you experience a mood swing between being overexcited and being depressed.

Symptoms of Depression

The following are some of the symptoms that characterize depression. However, these symptoms vary:

- » Anxiety
- » Helplessness
- » Worthlessness
- » Overeating or undereating
- » Irritability
- » Gaining or losing weight
- » Inability to concentrate
- » Loss of appetite
- » Feelings of extreme sadness
- » Insomnia
- » Difficulty making decisions

» Fatigue

» Loss of interest in things that the person used to enjoy

Causes of Depression

» Physiological factors

» Sociological factors

» Chemical imbalance

» Personality

Tips on How to Deal with Depression

» Seek spiritual help

» Seek professional help

» Group therapy

» Join a mastermind group

» Change your focus

» Develop a positive outlook

» Associate yourself with positive and enthusiastic people

The fact of the matter is that you cannot function at your best capacity when depressed. This is an illness that can potentially alienate you from your loved ones, close acquaintances, and the rest of the world. With accurate diagnosis, proper treatment, and self-help resources, you can overcome depression and live the life that you are meant to live. What does it take to transform frustration into creative opportunity and unlock the power to succeed? Let's talk next about that.

PART II

HOW TO TRANSFORM FRUSTRATION INTO CREATIVE
OPPORTUNITIES AND UNLOCK THE POWER TO SUCCEED

CHAPTER 9

CHANGING YOUR EXPECTATIONS

Whatever we expect with confidence becomes our own self-fulfilling prophecy."

Brain Tracy

Everywhere you turn to, and in every walk of life, you will discover that there are a lot of people whose expectations have not been fulfilled. You will also learn that most of their expectations are not congruent with their actions. Consequently, the unmet expectations have led to most people becoming victims of frustrations, depression, stress, and anxiety. Therefore transforming this emotional dysfunction into productivity and unlocking the power to succeed, the evaluation and change of your expectations are crucial.

Expectation Defined

The law of expectation states that "whatever you expect with confidence becomes your own self-fulfilling prophecy." With that in mind, let us now define expectation. Expectation is the act of looking forward to an event that is about to happen. It is a mental belief that something is going to happen in a particular way. It has much to do with how you feel. Usually, you get what you expect in life, and every experience (either negative or positive) builds your expectation. The expectation is built by what you focus on most of the time. It is, therefore, important to change your expectations if the outcomes you are producing are not in harmony with your expectations.

Expectation can be a powerful force in one's life. How can you use expectation as a force in your life? Can you expect good things to happen, and they will? George Bernard Shaw states, "Remember, our conduct is influenced not by our experience but by our expectations." Expectations drive much of what is happening around us. To turn frustration into productive opportunities, you have to change your expectation.

Frustration often indicates that your expectations are not realistic and that you need to readjust them to be congruent with your desired outcome. Do not allow frustration and anger to destroy everything you have worked for when your expectations are not met; rather, examine what was responsible for why your expectations were not met. This will produce positive results and move you in the right direction. Is it that the standard has been set too high or too low? Is the time frame realistic for the anticipated outcome? Is the action commensurate with the expected results? Your ability to respond to these questions will put you on the path to undeniable success.

Dr. John Maxwell stated, "We all deal with the impact of expectations in three dimensions; Expectations we have for ourselves, Expectations we have of others and Expectations others have of us." Often, these dimensions of expectation can be very frustrating if they are not realistic and crystal clear. To turn frustration into creative opportunities, you have to clarify expectations in every dimension and frequently revisit them to make adjustments or to realign your expectations to be congruent with what it is that you want.

One of the ways you can turn frustration into opportunity is to change your expectations. Norman Vincent Peale said, "We tend to get what we expect." Frustration occurs due to unrealistic goals and objectives, such as creating a lifestyle that is not achievable with the available resources. Conversely, when the expectation is not in harmony with the corresponding action, the anticipated end is not going to be attained. Einstein defined insanity as "doing the same things over and over again and expecting different results." Hence, if the outcome is not what you expected, you either have to change the actions producing your unwanted outcomes or change your expectation altogether.

We often have expectations for others. Most of the time, these are false expectations predicated on things that are superficial and superfluous. Frustration occurs when such expectations are not met. To change this emotional feeling, you have to change your expectation to conform to your appraisal of the situation or the person. For instance, if you wish to bring about a change in a friend, you have to change your expectation. Begin to expect that which you desire to happen, and you will note changes are occurring. Norman Vincent Peale said, "If you paint in your mind a picture of bright and happy expectations, you put yourself into a condition conducive to your goal."

What do you expect from those around you? What are the expectations for your activities? How do your expectations play a role in how you act? Paint the image of your expectations in your mind to create an atmosphere conducive for its achievement. For example, when a feeling of sadness and frustration occurs, paint a different picture in your mind to change that state of emotion, which will overtly utter your expectation.

Dennis Wholey said, "Expecting the world to treat you fairly because you are a good person is a little like expecting the bull not to attack you because you are a vegetarian." It is naive and unrealistic to expect people to treat you the way you want to be treated. There will always be people and events that will not meet your expectations. With that in mind, when you are frustrated because your expectations were not achieved, you must be ready to change your expectations accordingly. This action will eventually transform the negative outcome into productive opportunities and the ability to unlock the power to succeed.

Frustration from an expectation occurs when you have a particular belief, opinion, or feeling that people should behave a certain way, or events should follow a particular path. In this manner, you tend to focus exclusively on something that you want and forget to pay attention to what is happening. When you interact with others, you believe that you have been clear about targeted outcomes and that you are all on the same page. You may observe discrepancies, but you do not step in to adjust your expectations because of what you believe.

"When you expect things to happen – strangely enough – they do happen." (JP Morgan). Change your expectation and see your reality; your world changes to the degree that you desire it to change. Eventually, you will arrive at the place you aspired to be. Orison Swett Marden observed, "We advance on our journey only when we face our goal when we are confident and believe we are going to win out." Therefore, never underestimate the power of your expectations and those of the people around you. As a matter of fact, why don't you change those negative expectations right now? You might be surprised how your life will turn out and make remarkable outcomes possible beyond your wildest dreams.

Brian Tracy said that "winners make a habit of acquiring their own positive expectations in advance of the event." This could not be more accurate. To turn frustration into creative opportunities, it is imperative that you make it a habit to consistently create new and positive expectations before and after any event in your life. For instance, if you did not accomplish your anticipated goal, set new positive expectations, and immediately take action towards their realization.

Ways to Change Your Negative Expectation

Ralph Charell remarked, "Nobody succeeds beyond his or her wildest expectations unless he or she begins with some wild expectations." If you do not appreciate the outcomes of your life, you can change those outcomes. Don't take it from the naysayer that the changes that you espouse are unattainable. Here are a few tips on how to change your expectation:

Change What You Are Focusing On: What is your focus? Change your focus to change your expectation. If your outcome is not what you expected, you can alter that outcome by changing your focus to produce your desired expectation.

Change Your Belief System: Your belief system can empower or restrain you from the success that you envision in different aspects of your life. Changing a belief system that no longer serves you in the pursuit of your purpose will affect your overall expectations.

Develop a Clear Vision for Your Life: It's improbable to expect what you have not clearly defined. Consequently, to change your expectation, clearly define what your expectations are. This is one factor you cannot afford to neglect.

Disrupt the Patterns of Events by Altering the Process: If you intend to change your expectation, disrupt the process that creates the patterns of your negative expectation. Processes such as negative thinking habits and self-talk can produce unwanted expectation.

Learn the Dos and Don'ts: Do not apply the same strategy if it is not working. Learn the dos and don'ts in the process to change your expectations. In the process of living things are always changing, hence what worked yesterday may not necessarily work today. Your ability to ascertain the dos and don'ts in the process is invaluable in changing your expectations.

Enlist the Help of a Coach: Enlist the help of a coach to set a roadmap for realistic expectations. The help of a mentor is invaluable. This individual will hold you accountable for your actions and help you to find a course that meets your expectations.

Change Your Attitude: Your attitude plays an important role; thus, it's very significant in changing your negative expectations. A negative attitude toward your project will produce negative results. A positive attitude is key. Hence, having a positive mental attitude is invaluable in changing the expectation.

Take Action: The more action you take, the more progress you make. It does not matter how much you know until you start taking action to implement the acquired knowledge in the direction of your anticipated goal. Therefore, taking action is imperative in changing your expectation.

This list by no means is exhaustive. Create positive expectations by making sincere decisions. Nurture your expectations by never settling for anything less than what you desire. When you are frustrated due to unmet expectations, take action immediately, and apply these tips to transform frustration into creative opportunities and unlock the power to succeed.

CHANGING YOUR BELIEF SYSTEMS AND LET'S FOCUS ON THAT NEXT

CHAPTER 10

CHANGING YOUR BELIEF SYSTEMS

"Belief in yourself, belief in your abilities, will override fear almost every time. The only thing we are afraid of is what we are capable of accomplishing."

Rich DiGirolamo

What is Belief Systems

A belief system is a structured process by which we evaluate everything in our lives. We develop our belief system based on how we interpret the world around us according to our observations and experiences. Your beliefs can empower you or hold you back in many different ways. They can stop you from living the life of your dreams. Belief is so critical that it can even stop you from trusting that you are entitled to anything more than average life. If you are setting goals, making plans, and taking action, self-limiting beliefs can sabotage your success without you being aware that it is happening.

You cannot effectively change anything until you first identify what it is and then take action to affect the change that is anticipated. With that said, your first option is to identify your belief systems. I'm sure you have one, but you might be unsure of how it affects their lives. Whatever you believe or don't believe can sabotage your efforts or help turn your frustrations into productive opportunities. It is important to examine your belief system and identify beliefs that are empowering or limiting.

Some of the beliefs that you hold have been developed over some time because of what you have experienced in the past. It will be interesting to discover that some of your beliefs have nothing to do with your present reality. You hold on to them at the expense of your overall wellbeing. You have become used to them when faced with problems in your life, even if they have proven not to be productive in helping you reach a positive, growth-enhancing solution.

Michael Korda said, "To succeed, we must first believe that we can." Your beliefs shape your destiny and your actions, which is what you do and don't do. Your actions inevitably create the outcomes in your life and the circumstances you will have to deal with. Our value systems are what we regard as important, while our belief systems are truths that we hold to be self-evident. With that said, when your belief system is congruent with your desires, you create endless possibilities even when you meet uncertain conditions in the pursuit of your intents. Henry Ford observed, "Whether you believe you can do a thing or not, you are right." The beliefs that you hold shape your thinking pattern. If your thoughts are *can or can't*, either of them will become your reality.

Sumner Redstone says, "Success is not built on success. It's built on failure. It's built on frustration. Sometimes it's built on catastrophe." This understanding is pivotal for channeling your frustrations into productive opportunities and unlocking the power to succeed. Your belief system is the actual set of perceptions from which you live your daily life. If your belief system indicates that you cannot achieve your objectives or your anticipated outcome, you certainly will not achieve it no matter how hard you'd try. The problem that you encounter from time to time is an indication that your belief will fail if you do not adjust them as you grow.

Napoleon Hill observed, "Whatever the mind of a man can conceive and believe it can achieve." You have to occasionally reassess your values to see if those rules of old still fit your current life and direction. These old values were put in place to keep you safe and get you started on the next leg of your journey. They allow you to process, categorize, and file new information in a logical and orderly fashion. Such values keep you from doing things that, at that time, are dangerous to you emotionally, mentally, or physically. As you grow, mature, and learn, you can gradually handle more of what life hands you. It is then that you must be able to reassess your values to get rid of old and unnecessary beliefs that are no longer congruent with your current level of life and put in place new ones that can allow you move forward in life.

As human beings, we are usually confronted with fear when the subject of change occurs. It is the fear of the unknown because you are attempting an undertaking that is outside of what you previously set up as boundaries for your safe anchorage. At this moment, you can feel misplaced if you do not have some knowledge or new belief to put in its place. Overcoming the fear of change involves accepting that your beliefs will change over time and then taking control of the change so that it occurs at your pace. Evaluate your current position and adjust your beliefs as needed.

There are two types of beliefs: empowering beliefs and self-limiting beliefs. The one that dominates is the one that is most fed. It is that which you focus on most of the time that becomes your reality. If you feed your self-limiting beliefs most of the time, they will dominate your life and manifest in your actions. Empowering beliefs come from the perspective of possibility; these are sets of values that motivate you to take consistent action irrespective of the odds against you. Empowering beliefs include: if you believe you can, you can; if you believe it's possible, it's possible; if you believe it's attainable, it's attainable.

Self-limiting beliefs are certain ideas that you have picked up from your family, peers, teachers, friends, the media, your environment, and other influences. Self-limiting beliefs include: I am not good enough; I am not worthy; I will never become anything; I need to be of a certain cultural background to have a decent job; I am from the wrong side of town.

To turn frustrations into productive opportunities, you must get rid of self-limiting beliefs that don't serve your purpose and adopt empowering beliefs that will eventually serve you in achieving your anticipated objectives.

Tips on Changing Belief Systems

Limiting beliefs are negative thoughts and images that have been drilled into your head by others. Changing them will enhance your chances for success in overcoming frustrations. Changing some of your negatives beliefs will require you to reprogram your hard drive. The following suggestions will put you on the path of changing your belief system:

Change Your Associations: This will prove to be a painful experience, but the rewards are tremendous. I do not by any means suggest that you change these associations abruptly, but it is important that you begin to eliminate associations that are not congruent with your reality.

Identify the Origin: Get to the root of these negative beliefs and deal with them from that perspective. If you address these beliefs from the surface, you will only succeed in stopping them in the interim; over time, they will resurface. Thus, it is important to identify the origin and make the changes from that point.

Read Good Books: Read material that will support your expectations. That will spur you into action. Charlie Tremendous Jones said, "You will be the same person in five years as you are today except for the people you meet and the books you read." This will help alter some of the belief systems that have held you captive over the years.

Find a Mentor: Everyone needs a mentor at some point in his or her life. A mentor is one who is considered to be wise, trustworthy, serves as a model, offers counsel when asked, believes in lending a helping hand to others, tries to maintain a positive attitude, and encourages others' efforts. A mentor builds trust, exchanges ideas, always maintains confidentiality, and facilitates growth.

Seminars: Attending seminars at least three times a year will help realign your belief system because you will become exposed to new information that will alter your view. This, in turn, will affect your beliefs. For instance, you have the belief that you cannot become. However, seminars tailored in the direction of your specific needs can help change those limiting belief systems.

Self-examination: Frequent self-evaluation is of inestimable value. As we interact daily, we tend to imbibe ideas, habits, and thought patterns that are not in harmony with our core values and expectations. Robert Xerox wondered why his belief system kept producing negative thoughts, so he decided to evaluate himself to find out what the problem was. Thus, self-examination can help to detoxify the impurity that can affect your beliefs negatively.

Spend More Time with Positive People: It is said that your associations determine your destination. If you must stay positive and enthusiastic, you must spend more time with positive people. In other to change your limiting beliefs, you have to surround yourself with positive people who can influence you with their positive ideas. Stay away from the naysayers.

Take Action: Another problem is inaction. Having acquired the information, it is important to understand that if consistent action is not taken, the desired outcomes will not come to fruition. Take action to correct limiting beliefs by doing what you should bring the anticipated expectation. Valuable how-to knowledge will be unproductive unless acted upon.

CHANGING YOUR ATTITUDE AND THAT'S EXACTLY WHERE WE ARE GOING NEXT.

CHAPTER 11
CHANGING YOUR ATTITUDE

"Character cannot be developed in ease and quiet. Only through experience of trial and suffering can the soul be strengthened, vision cleared, ambition inspired, and success achieved."

Helen Keller

Attitude Defined

Attitude can be defined as the way that a person views life or tends to behave towards it. It is the position in any given circumstance that produces an outstanding character. Merriam Webster defines attitude as "an internal position or feeling about something else." A positive mental attitude gives you the confidence to approach any situation with the belief that you will achieve your goal. Having a positive attitude can increase achievement through optimism. The mind continues to seek ways to win in spite of the circumstances.

Attitude is everything. Attitudes, whether positive or negative, have the power to impact the success of an individual or an organization profoundly. Attitudes are contagious. Attitudes impact the bottom line and affect your every thought and the results that your thoughts bring. Positive mental attitude is indispensable in today's competitive marketplace as well as in your endeavors. It has become imperative to develop and maintain a positive mental attitude regardless of the circumstances.

A positive mental attitude is everything, regardless of what occupation or responsibilities you have. Most people are frustrated because change is constantly impacting everyone. While you may not be able to change the circumstances around you, you can change yourself. Sometimes, that changes everything, because you have control over yourself and can make choices that will move you in the right direction. Developing new and improved attitudes can turn frustration into creative opportunities. When you change from a negative to a positive attitude, you will stop allowing frustration to destroy your dream and embrace it as an opportunity to go from good to great.

In his book *Daily Motivations for African-America*, Dennis Kimbro states, "Your attitude toward your potential is either the key to or the lock on the door of personal achievement." It is not what you go through or what happens to you that is relevant to your achievements, but how you respond to it. It is the attitude toward the situation that determines if you will be able to transform frustration into creative opportunities. For example, working on a major project will require a positive attitude. It is how you respond to the situation that will ultimately help you deal with the challenges.

Changing your negative attitude cannot be emphasized enough, because it is at the core of who you are and what you do. Your attitude, whether positive or negative, will greatly affect the outcome of any given tasks. If your mental attitude is something that can't be done, you will fall short of your anticipated outcome, which will lead to frustration. In other words, to transform frustration into creative opportunity, it is imperative to change your attitude. In other words to transform frustration into creative opportunity is imperative to change or readjust your attitude before and after to position yourself with the right frame of mind before you embark on the project or any endeavor for that matter.

Zig Ziglar observed, "You cannot tailor-make the situations in life, but you can tailor-make the attitudes to fit those situations." People with negative attitudes are frustrated at any given opportunity. They seldom expect good things to happen to them. These individuals are often stressed, always embracing the worst possible outcome; their negative attitude becomes a self-fulfilling prophecy. To unlock the power to succeed, you must not allow people or situations in life to determine your attitude. Develop the habit of having a positive attitude.

Your attitude is YOUR CHOICE! Irrespective of what you go through in life, your attitude must be your decision, not someone else's. Most of the time, you allow people and events to choose your attitude; this can be detrimental to your transforming frustration into creative opportunities. The right mental attitude will negate any frustration. With the right attitude, you will see frustration as challenges and as opportunities that will move you to the next level of experience. Developing the right attitude and the appropriate state of mind is a must in turning frustration into outstanding opportunities.

Sidlow Baxter said, "What is the difference between an obstacle and an opportunity? – Your attitude." Twelve spies were sent to spy out the land, and the group became two as they reported back home. Ten out the twelve saw giants, while the remaining two saw land that flowed with milk and honey. What sets these men apart? Their attitude sets them apart. When you are confronted with a frustrating situation, it is your attitude that helps you make the best of it. You understand that in every frustrating situation, there is an opportunity to be, do, and have what will take you to the next level of life.

Tips on Developing a Positive Attitude

Change your attitude to transform frustration into creative opportunities and unlock the power to succeed.

- » Associate with positive people
- » Learn to put things into perspective
- » Read and listen to informative and inspirational material
- » Use positive self-affirmation
- » Set goals and develop a detailed plan for achieving them
- » Develop solution-oriented thinking
- » Focus on the ideal outcome
- » Build and maintain your self-confidence
- » Build and maintain a positive self-image

Nothing, absolutely nothing, contributes more to your ability to transform frustration into creative opportunities and see possibilities in every challenge than your attitude. The fact of the matter is that anyone, including you, can develop and maintain a positive attitude.

NOW, LET'S FOCUS ON THE NEXT SUBJECT,
AND THAT'S TRANSFORMING YOUR THOUGHTS

CHAPTER 12

TRANSFORMING YOUR THOUGHTS

"It is hardly possible to build anything if frustration, bitterness, and a mood of helplessness prevail."

Lech Walesa

A man becomes what he thinks. The driving force or motive behind his course of action is what he thinks; his thoughts attract him to his circumstances and environment; what a man thinks determines what type of friends and companions will gather around him; what a man thinks decides whether he will be happy or miserable, successful or unsuccessful, healthy or unhealthy, prosperous or poverty-stricken, hated or loved. What a man thinks either builds up his character or pulls it down. What a man thinks can overcome fate or strengthen it, can align him with his purpose and destiny, or make him an outcast and a wanderer in deserted places.

Indeed, there is no limit to the power of thought because it is a power of inexhaustible potency. It is this power that distinguishes man from animal; it is this power by which he can mount up to God; it is the power that can make the unsuccessful successful in the battlefields of life; it is the power that can make the loftiest achievement possible; it is the power by which he can overcome difficulties, how you think impacts the quality of your work, your productivity, and your relationships.

The mind is capable of producing countless thoughts in a day. There are no neutral thoughts—they are either positive or negative, making or breaking you, progressive or retrogressive. The biggest deterrent to success is the Negative Mind, which most often is the product of frustration. It's of importance and in your interest to control your thoughts, because thoughts have its consequences. Romans 12:2 states, "And be not conformed to this world: but be ye transformed by the renewing of your mind, that ye may prove what is that good, and acceptable, and perfect, will of God." Start training your mind to think positive thoughts, which are good, acceptable, and perfect in spite of the circumstances. You are a product of your thoughts; if you think it long enough, you live according to the pattern of thought that you maintain, for as a man thinketh in his heart, so is he.

To think the solution is to create solutions. Thoughts are the core of who you are; therefore, examine your thoughts wisely to have a clear understanding of who you are. Your ability to think initiates action from your mind. Thinking is a process that can be set off by the experience, need, lack, or determination to achieve change. To think is to consider, reflect, ponder, and analyze. Thinking results in opinion formation, assessment, and judgment. The essence of thinking is to foster guidance in making choices. Thinking is a natural process that makes humans superior to animals. The human brain functions instinctively from life experiences. The mind of man is the storehouse of experiences, studies, and an archive on which the brain relies for thought processes.

When an event sparks negative thoughts, you may experience fear, insecurity, anxiety, depression, rage, and guilt, worthlessness, helplessness, and frustration. This emotional disposition leads to disorientation in whatever event is occurring in your life at that time. The most effective way to eliminate negative thoughts is to replace them with positive ones. Feed your mind with motivating and empowering thoughts that support your goals and expectations.

Change Your Mental Focus

Mental focus is the general term used to describe a person's thought processes. To transform frustrations into creative opportunities and unlock the power to succeed, you have to change your mental focus. For instance, when frustrating events occur, there is always this tendency to focus on the negative outcome, which in turn reinforces frustration. By taking control of your mental focus and focusing on the desired expectation, you can master frustration and transform it into a creative opportunity.

Dealing with your negative thoughts and how you see things can help reduce stress and turn frustration into opportunities. Thinking *solution thoughts* helps you stop a negative thought, thus helping to eliminate frustration. In the same light, negating irrational thoughts helps you to avoid exaggerating the negative thought, anticipating the worst, and interpreting an event or circumstances incorrectly. Your thoughts are like baits that a fisherman uses to catch fish.

Each type of bait determines the type of fish to be caught. In the same token, if your thoughts are negative, they will attract negative outcomes.

The Bible tells us that "As a man thinketh in his so is he." (Proverbs 23:7a) Everything begins with your thoughts. "You become what you think about the most." We are a summation of our thoughts put together. As you encounter difficulty in any area of your life, instead of thinking regarding the problems, think regarding the solutions. This will turn your frustrations into possibilities. Thoughts create your identity, your reality, and your destiny.

When you are problem-oriented, focusing on the difficulties and engaging in self-defeating behaviors amplifies the situation, which is ultimately blown out of proportion. Turning frustration into creative opportunities requires you to think regarding the solution. What you dwell on most becomes that which controls you. If you dwell long enough on the solutions to the problem, it will become that which will ultimately guide you and your actions.

Solution-oriented people are always looking for ways to solve problems or whatever is responsible for their frustration. They ask themselves empowering questions such as how they can solve the problem and what they can change to yield a different result? When all of the information has been gathered, the most important aspect of the process begins: TAKE ACTION to deal with the situation, turning it to a productive outcome that will benefit you. Problem-oriented people are engrossed with their problems and whine about their frustration all day long, contaminating everyone around them. Instead of seeking alternative solutions to the problems, they amplify it.

I'll never make it! There's no way! I know I can't! Never. No. Can't— the thoughts you provide in your mind are the seeds that will produce after their kind. All self-limiting thoughts of weakness, failure, unhappiness, or poverty are detrimental and self-destructive, to say the least, if allowed taking residence in your mind. These thoughts are enemies, giants attempting to hinder your present and future progress toward your aspiration for an extraordinary life. The key is to strategically counterattack and slay those giants whenever they try to take control of your mind. They are the most devious self-fulfilling prophecy, stealing your very ability to succeed.

Thinking solutions will help transform frustration into creative opportunities and unlock your power to succeed. Do not yield to negative thinking, as this will produce more frustrations in your life.

CHANGING YOUR CONFESSION AND THAT'S EXACTLY WHERE WE ARE GOING NEXT.

CHAPTER 13

CHANGING YOUR CONFESSION

———————⋅◦∾⨯◅⋅———————

Everything is stagnant right now. I feel something is getting ready to be reborn because there's lot of frustration.

Bernie Worrell

Words are very powerful; they have a greater impact than most care to admit. What you say can set the tone for the direction of your life. Words can lift you out of a difficult situation or keep you bound. You can have what you SAY! With words, you can create images in your mind's eye; consequently, it is important to speak the right words to create the right image of who you want to be, what you want to achieve, and where you want to be. The words you are speaking help change your vision. Most of the time, it is what you see that is the source of your frustration, but you are not obliged to align with the negative outcome that you see. You can begin to confess what it is that you want to see as the outcome, so changing your confession or communication is invaluable in transforming frustration.

Inner Communication: This is the dialogue that you are having with yourself. This type of communication manifests in your actions, that is, what you do and don't. Inner dialogue tends to amplify your frustration if it is negative and not congruent with your core values. Allowing your inner dialogue to focus on the negative outcomes is detrimental to your success, and it produces frustration. Changing your inner communication from disempowering to empowering words can redirect your frustration into a creative opportunity.

Romans 10:10 reveals that the Greek word for "confess" is *homologeo*, a combination of *Homos* meaning "same" and *lego* meaning to "to speak." *Homologeo*, therefore, means, "to speak the same thing as another." In our case, *homologeo* means, "saying the same thing God says." From the definition above, to confess means "to speak the same thing as another." To overcome frustration, you have to stop rehearsing the negatives in your life. When you rehearse your weaknesses, you are speaking the same thing as another, another being what your present reality or situation is saying. This creates a picture that is not in harmony with your core values and expectations.

If you confess with your mouth: This indicates speaking the same thing as another. Beware of this, because you become what you confess. Hence, it is imperative that you must confess with your mouth what God's Word says about you; when you do that, you agree with God and His Word. To obtain results, you need to believe in your heart what your mouth is confessing. The scripture tells us that ".for out of the abundance of the heart the mouth speaketh" (Matthew 12:34). This implies that your mouth is the gateway of your heart; hence, whatever proceeds out of your mouth should be in harmony with what is in your heart.

This is where a lot of people are missing it, and that is, confessing with the mouth without necessarily believing with the hearts. It is imperative, therefore, to know that there is a connection between what comes out of the mouth and what the heart believes. This combination works perfectly well and achieves results.

How do you talk to yourself? Do you use the words "can't," "won't," or "don't?" Many people do. Do you find that what you say to yourself turns out to be true? Even in the heat of battle, an affirmation of word builds the right images. Use empowering words when you talk to yourself to alter the state of your mind and your overall perspective. We can reach a new level of living if we feed ourselves empowering words and practice saying them until they become a habit.

Proverbs 18:21 states, "Death and life are in the power of the tongue, and they that love it shall eat the fruit thereof." Words can be empowering or disempowering. Consequently, remember that the words you use to empower yourself will have a lasting effect if you practice them. It takes at least 21 days to develop a habit. After a week, you will see that it becomes easier. It's a mindset, and you can control it with your thoughts. Be proactive and not reactive—give yourself some good words.

Proverbs 6:2 states, "Thou art snared with the words of thy mouth, Thou art taken with the words of thy mouth." Now that's a very strong indictment. It means that you are enslaved by your own words, imprisoned by the words that you speak. Most people tend to speak negatively about themselves, other people, or situations when things do not happen the way they anticipated. One of the ways to amplify frustration is through the negative dialogue that you are having with yourself.

Norman Vincent Peale observed, "Watch your manner of speech if you wish to develop a peaceful state of mind. Start each day by affirming peaceful, contented, and happy attitudes, and your days will tend to be pleasant and successful." Therefore, to transform frustration, you have to replace negative words with positive affirmations, words that affirm your core values, and what you want.

Anthony Robbins states, "The way we communicate with others and with ourselves ultimately determines the quality of our lives." This could not be more accurate. Your ultimate success depends largely on the way that you communicate personally and professionally. Your ability to communicate effectively with yourself and with others who can assist in difficult times is key to overcoming frustration, opening doors of new opportunities, and unlocking the power to succeed.

THE NEXT SUBJECT WE ARE GOING TO BE LOOKING AT IS THE POWER OF PERSONAL DEVELOPMENT.

CHAPTER 14

THE POWER OF PERSONAL DEVELOPMENT

"The big challenge is to become all that you have the possibility of becoming. You cannot believe what it does to the human spirit to maximize your human potential and stretch yourself to the limit."

Jim Rohn

What Is Personal Development

P ersonal development is a lifelong pursuit because life is a work in progress. There will never be a day when you will not require dedication, discipline, and commitment to your values, plans, and actions. You are capable of continually improving every aspect of your life. Each day provides the opportunity to either advance or retreat in the pursuit of your destiny. Personal development is not a destination but a journey.

We will concentrate on seven areas of personal development: spirit, body, mind, finances, family, career, and social life. One or more of these areas is often ravaged with frustration. The ability to transform frustration into creative opportunities and unlock the power to succeed is predicated on your consistent evolvement in these areas. Jim Rohn says, "Work harder on yourself than you do on your job." In the same vein, we could say "work harder on yourself than you do on others." We have seen many people become frustrated because of their poor people skills. Relationships between spouses or colleagues can be frustrating because you are trying so hard to work on others rather than working on yourself.

"If you work hard on your job you'll make a living; if you work hard on yourself, you'll make a fortune," Says Jim Rohn. "Fortune" does not only means finances but also knowledge, friendship, skill, and virtue. Some governing values include a relationship with God, family, health, friends, education, work, loving relationships, financial security, and emotional well-being. It is important to reiterate that part of your personal development is to know with whom you spend your time because this determines who you will ultimately become. So choose your friends wisely. Birds of a feather flock together. If you scratch with the turkeys, you'll never fly with the eagles.

If you are frustrated in your career, for instance, you could spend time with the top people in your field. Choose role models and reading books to gain wisdom. One of the keys to personal development is to follow the leaders, not the followers.

Effects of Personal Development

You are designed for optimum performance. You possess the limitless capacity to demonstrate power and excellence in any sphere of life. Consequently, personal development is the process by which you enhance and maximize your intellectual and spiritual abilities to enhance your self-worth. It also enables you to maximize your potential and minimize your liabilities.

In your personal development, it is what you choose to listen to, watch, or read that enhances your understanding of your life and teaches you what you need to do to succeed. To transform frustration into creative opportunities and unlock the power to succeed, you have to focus on continual personal growth and development. Read books, listen to tapes, take courses, watch videos, study, and attend workshops. This will provide you with unforgettable learning experiences.

There are some of the domino effects of personal development. For these effects to occur, the process must have direction and purpose, and its foundation must be predicated on your core values. You cannot afford to go off on a tangent on this endeavor.

Personal Development:

- » Gives you a positive self-image
- » Enhances your belief system
- » Helps create positive self-awareness
- » Increases your participatory role in events and activities
- » Qualifies you for promotion and advancement
- » Optimizes your leadership capabilities
- » Develops your gifts

» Enables you to accept and manage criticism

» Liberates you from cultural dogmatism

» Develops personal confidence and confidence in others

» Enables you to harness your potential

» Updates and upgrades your inner technologies

In his book, *Imitation is Limitation,* John Mason states, "The quality of your life will be in direct proportion to a commitment to excellence, regardless of what you choose to do." You are responsible for your personal development; hence, it is imperative that you have to begin your personal growth and development today to experience these twelve domino effects and many more.

The Power of Self-improvement

"People seldom improve when they have no other model but themselves to copy after," said Oliver Goldsmith. Kaizen is a Japanese management term referring to constant, continuous, and never-ending improvement. Anthony Robbins calls this concept Constant And Never Ending Improvement (CANI). Kaizen is a way of life. It is a constant improvement in every aspect of your life. You have a built-in mechanism to grow and to improve. Therefore, ascertaining how to improve your relationship, knowledge, attitude, goals, and goal-setting strategies, leadership skills, and time management should be your daily responsibility. Experts in the field of human development say that everything can be improved by at least ten percent.

There is no pursuit more venerable than the pursuit of self-improvement. Self-improvement begins with your spirit, mind, and body. Everything is capable of being improved, even if only incrementally. The concept of continuous improvement can be applied to every aspect of your personal and professional life. The consistent and constant pursuit of improvement in all areas of your life is indispensable in the attainment of your true potential. Hence, improving daily, whether by spending some time exercising, reading, visualizing, or forging better relationships, you are evolving toward the desired end.

The mark of virtually every top achiever is a daily dedication to improvement in both personal and professional life. To be effective, you have to do things daily and consistently to advance in the direction of your goals. One of the enemies you will have to deal with is frustration. There will be moments when it seems impossible to move forward toward your goals. Your consistent dedication to personal improvement is pivotal in your transforming frustration into creative opportunities and unlocking the power to succeed.

Brian Tracy remarked, "If you wish to achieve worthwhile things in your personal and career life, you must become a worthwhile person in your self-development." It is fundamental to apply the Kaizen or CANI principles consistently to every component of your life, from spiritual to physical, business to family, to attain peak performance as you migrate toward your desired end. George Bernard Shaw said, "People are always blaming their circumstances for what they are. I don't believe in circumstances. The people who get on in this world are the people who get up and look for the circumstances they want, and if they can't find them make them." This is a bold declaration. You must not settle for the circumstances that life serves you, including frustrating circumstances. You have the innate capacity to create the circumstances that are conducive for your growth and the achievement of your goals.

CHANGING YOUR FOCUS,
THAT'S EXACTLY WHERE WE ARE GOING NEXT.

CHAPTER 15

CHANGING YOUR FOCUS

When you allow yourself to begin to dream big dreams, creatively abandon the activities that are taking up too much of your time, and focus your inward energies on alleviating your main constraints, you start to feel an incredible sense of power and confidence.

Brian Tracy

What you are focusing on eventually get magnified, consequently it is imperative that you give a lot of consideration to what you are focusing on. It is important that you understand that life does not always happen to us as anticipated. Therefore focusing on the negative outcomes and unfavorable conditions in your life will lead to bouts of heartaches and frustration in your personal and professional life. The quest, therefore of overcoming and transforming frustration into productivity and unlock the power to succeed requires a change of focus.

Focus Defined

- » To give attention to one particular subject, situation, or person
- » To adapt or adjust so that things can be seen clearly
- » To aim rays of light onto a particular point using a lens
- » Point at which an object must be situated so that a well-defined image of it may be produced.

Oxford Dictionary

To focus is to clear your mind of what is out of your control, to focus on and act upon your goals and objectives. For many people, the idea of focusing on what you want and attracting it in your life seems unreal. With all of the negative misinformation from the media and friends, it's easier to dwell on the negative aspects of life and get frustrated than to focus on the numerous positive things in your lives. This is all about focusing on a particular objective long enough to produce a defined reality. The objective could be anything. For instance, if you focus on a particular desire, whether negative or positive, it will produce the desire. Whatever you concentrate on grows in your life. If the outcome of your project is frustrating, change that outcome by changing what you are focusing on to produce a different outcome.

A clear, intentional focus moves you towards your dreams quickly and effectively. When you have too much on the go at the same time, you often end up attempting your hand at many different things. You become a jack of all trades and a master of none. As a result, you do not produce the results that you desire. You may feel frustrated because of the stress of being pulled in many directions, leaving you exhausted and unable to move forward.

Most people speak more about what they don't want than what they do want. The idea is that focusing on what you do *not* want makes it happen. For example, focusing on not making mistakes causes you to make mistakes. Focusing on not finishing a project before its deadline makes you unable to finish.

Anthony Robbins observed, "One reason, so few of us achieve what we truly want is that we never direct our focus; we never concentrate our power. Most people dabble their way through life, never deciding to master anything in particular." I cannot emphasize this enough: when you focus on what you don't want in your life that is the exact reality that will manifest. Consequently, it is crucial that you are focusing exactly on what you want in your personal and professional life.

Incredible Power of Focus in Your Life

The power of focus is a rare skill today. By developing your ability to focus, you will be empowered to transform frustration into opportunities, enhance your productivity, and unlock the power to succeed. Where you place, your focus is where the rest of your mind and emotions will follow. When you focus on the negative events in your life, you will attract more negative events. The Bible says that "everything produces after its kind." This means that every positive thought will produce positive outcomes, while negative thoughts will produce negative outcomes. Hence, when you focus on the positive things in your life, you will eventually produce more positive things in your life; in the same light, negative things in your life will produce more of the same.

It is imperative that in any challenge or difficulty you encounter, your focus must be solution-oriented, not problem-oriented. If your focus is negative, replace it with a positive. Instead of dwelling on the things that are missing in your life and the negative outcomes, focus on what you already have and what's possible in the future. This is one of the skills that most successful individuals have habitually nurtured in their lives to enable them to achieve extraordinary results. People with the clarity of focus know exactly what they want and can function regardless of the frustrating events or people around them.

Discover what matters most to you, and then focus on that. Assess your values. Anything that is not congruent can be eradicated out of your life. This gives you more time to focus on what is important. Scrutinize the items on your schedule and delete anything that is no longer rewarding. Eliminate any activities that no longer please you or that no longer offer you value for the time spent. Focus on the 20% activities that will yield 80% of the results.

How to Deal With Frustration

Focus on Getting the Outcomes You Want: To turn frustration into creative opportunities, learn how to focus on your desired outcome. Recognize what you are focusing on and then be crystal clear about what you *want* to focus on it. This will enormously alter your state of frustration and turn it into a creative opportunity.

Focus on WHY: Examine the driving force behind your actions, the ultimate reason for doing what you are doing. When frustration steps in, you've got to assess the WHY and focus on it. You may be on the verge of giving up on your dreams because of frustration. What will keep you motivated is focusing on WHY.

Focus on Success: We often lose sight of our goals because of negative outcomes. By learning to focus on success, you will achieve better outcomes. When you focus on success, you are focusing on what you want and choosing that relevant course of action that will move you in the direction of your goal. Focusing on success takes into account that failure is inevitable; it is not a person but an event that occurred in your pursuit of success. This understanding will empower you to transform your frustration into opportunities and unlock the power to succeed.

Focus on Your Expectation: What is it that you want to accomplish? Focusing on your anticipated outcome will help you navigate through the events and difficulties that are responsible for your frustration. Do not focus on your desired outcome in moments of frustration. Concentrating on your outcome can become an incentive that will motivate you to take further action, finding answers to the challenges at hand, and tenaciously holding on to what you believe.

Focus On Your Potential: Potential is everything that you can be but have not become, how far you can go but have not yet gone, what you can achieve but have not yet accomplished. Every human being can be, do, and have, but too many people focus on their weaknesses, which produces frustration. To ignore one's weaknesses is to be naïve; however, you must focus on harnessing your potential to do what you need to do and acquire the results that you anticipate.

Focus on Your Positive Attitude: Attitude is everything. Your attitude before and after any objective is paramount to your success, whether personal or professional. When frustration sets in because you have not achieved your anticipated outcome or you are unable to meet a work deadline or your spouse is not responding in the manner, you are expecting, or the environment that you work in is toxic to the meaningful working relationship a positive mental attitude will serve you well. Therefore, focus on your attitude as much as possible.

Focus on What Is Working: You have to pay more attention to the things that are working positively in any endeavor and change those things that are not working. Too many people focus most of their resources on things that are not productive in their lives; this leads to frustration. To change and transform that negative energy into something useful, focus on what is working, and refine it to work better.

Focus on the Lesson Learned: With every undertaking, there are always lessons to learn, whether it was a positive or negative outcome. Life is a compilation of lessons learned. It is imperative that you focus on the lessons learned rather than focusing on the negative outcome. This will give you a proper perspective on how to take further action toward the realization of your goals and expectations. You want to pay close attention to the lessons that your experiences afford, as it will serve your purpose in future endeavors.

Focus on your Personal Growth: Achieving personal growth requires dedication to the process of growth. Therefore, focusing on your personal growth is invaluable to transform frustration into creative opportunities and unlock the power to succeed. Personal growth involves improving your attitude and acquiring new skills to deal with the challenges in your personal and professional life. Your personal growth entails a desire to change, the discipline to practice new behaviors, the determination to persist until you achieve your anticipated outcome, and the decision to take congruent action daily.

PERSEVERE! PERSEVERE! PERSEVERE! THAT'S OUR NEXT POINT OF CALL.

CHAPTER 16
PERSEVERE! PERSEVERE! PERSEVERE!

"Nothing in the world can take the place of persistence. Talent will not; nothing is more common than unsuccessful men with talent. Genius will not; unrewarded genius is almost a proverb. Education will not; the world is full of educated derelicts. Persistence and determination are omnipotent."

Calvin Coolidge

Perseverance Defined

Perseverance means commitment, hard work, patience, and endurance. This is not a quick fix, but rather staying focused until the anticipated expectation is attained. It is also being able to face difficulties calmly and without complaint. Perseverance means trying again and again. It is an important ingredient in maintaining a positive mental attitude in all aspects of your life. One of the foundational truths in the Holy Scriptures is that those who persist in sowing seed eventually bear fruit. Lack of perseverance translates into failure, despair, and ultimately, frustration, no matter the task at hand.

Perseverance is at the core of your ability to decide what you want, to take action, and to persevere through all obstacles and difficulties until you achieve your expectation. This is a critical determinant in your ability to transform frustration into creative opportunities and unlock your power to succeed. You may be frustrated with your initial outcomes. This is where a lot of people quit. Just because you came up short does not mean that your goal is unattainable; you may have to persevere until you have achieved it. You might learn invaluable lessons if you hang in there.

Perseverance is one of the roadmaps for success in any endeavor. It is a desirable quality that can be developed by anyone in pursuit of personal and professional success. As you pursue your dream, you will certainly run into somebody or something that hinders your progress. This is part of life. Those who persevere will prevail. Staying power will take you anywhere you wish to go. The power of perseverance cannot be overstated. After all, you cannot fail unless you quit before succeeding, for quitters never win, and winners never quit. Consequently, remember that the ability to endure delay without becoming frustrated and to persevere calmly when faced with difficulties is a prerequisite for success in any enterprise.

George Allen observed, "One of the most difficult things everyone has to learn is that for your entire life you must keep fighting and adjusting if you hope to survive. No matter who you are or what your position is, you must keep fighting for whatever it is you desire to achieve." Perseverance is the breakfast of champions. There cannot be any meaningful outcome without persevering through the numerous odds that wait for you on the path of life. Most people give up too soon and too easily when they are frustrated with negative people and situation. This is no small measure will hinder you from tapping into opportunities. Lack of perseverance is one of the major reasons why people are unfulfilled. This substantiated the admonition of Sir Winston Churchill when he said, "Never, never, never, never give up."

Brian Tracy discovered that "Sometimes your greatest asset is simply your ability to stay with it longer than anyone else." Many people quit too soon because of temporary detours. When everything else proves to be unfruitful, one of your greatest assets is your ability to be persistent. George E. Allen stated, "People of mediocre ability sometimes achieve outstanding success because they don't know when to quit. Most men succeed because they are determined to." That's you: be determined to live to your full potential.

Thomas Edison observed, "Many of life's failures are by people who did not realize how close they were to success when they gave up." To fail is not enough to quit; it is not an indication that success is unachievable. Thomas Edison described his perseverance: "When I have fully decided that a result is worth getting, I go ahead on it and make trial after trial until it comes." Most people become frustrated and give up when they fail. Persistence is the antidote to frustration.

"We can do anything we want to if we stick to it long enough," said Helen Keller. Perseverance takes discipline. There are things you may not feel like doing, but it takes discipline to do what you know you need to do. This can result in frustration; knowing what to do is crucial in this regard. Most people do not know exactly what to do. You have read this far, so you are interested in finding out what to do. Make a list. Next, find the determination to do what is on the list. This is the most difficult part: finding the positive self-discipline to do what you know you need to do. We all wrestle with discipline, for it does not come easily, not even for the most successful.

Men are not built in the absence of challenges; neither are they validated by the intensity of the challenges that face them. By persevering, they achieve amazing results. Thomas Carlyle stated that "permanence, perseverance, and persistence in spite of all obstacles, discouragement, and impossibilities: It is this that in all things distinguishes the strong soul from the weak." Frustration is common to the weak and the strong, but you can translate it to creative opportunities and unlock the power to succeed that makes the difference.

In his book, *Goals! How to get everything you want faster than you ever thought possible*, Brian Tracy, wrote that your ability to persist longer than anyone else is the quality that will guarantee great success. Lord Chesterfield further observed that "a man of sense is never discouraged by difficulties; he redoubles his industry and his diligence, he perseveres and infallibly prevails at last." Resolve in advance that you will never give up on your dreams when frustration occurs.

"Consider the postage stamp, my son. It secures success through its ability to stick to one thing till it gets there," remarked Josh Billings. Just has the stamp secures success through its ability to stick, in like manner will achieve your goals and objective when you persevere. Unless you persevere in your efforts, there will not be adequate time to go through the learning curves. Man has the innate capacity to persevere as long as he remains focused on his ultimate goal. Kin Hubbard stated, "There is no failure except in no longer trying. There is no defeat except within, no real insurmountable barrier, save our own inherent weakness of purpose." You become frustrated and give in to defeat when you resign to the prevailing circumstances in your life. This should not be so. When you persevere through it all, you will ultimately unlock the power to succeed and translate any frustrating event into opportunities to achieve extraordinary things.

Anthony Robbins observed, "People who fail to achieve their goals usually get stopped by frustration. They allow frustration to keep them from taking the necessary actions that would support them in achieving their desire. You get through this roadblock by plowing through frustration, taking each setback as the feedback you can learn from, and pushing ahead. I doubt you'll find many successful people who have not experienced this. All successful people learn that success is buried on the other side of frustration." Given a choice, I know you will choose to *transform your frustration into creative opportunities and unlock the power to succeed.* Go for it.

FINAL WORD

This book is not meant to answer all of the questions with regards to the frustration. I hope to challenge you not to abort your purpose due to frustration and empower you to transform frustration into creative opportunities and unlock the power to succeed.

At some point, we have all experienced frustration. Frustration results from different things and ranges from mild to severe. Frustration has always been looked at from a negative standpoint, but this book presents simple strategies for transforming frustration into creative opportunities, possibilities, and to unlocking the power to succeed.

Frustration thrives; you experience it daily, whether at home or work. That said, frustration does not present immediate problems or challenges. However, some can disorient you momentarily. How you interpret and respond to the experience determines if you will transform frustration into creative opportunities and unlock the power to succeed.

Follow the strategies in this book instead of allowing yourself to be defeated. You will be able to transform your frustrations into creative opportunities and unlock the power to succeed in every aspect of your life, personally and professionally.

THANK YOU

A Big thank you to you for purchasing and downloading my book and reading it to the end. If you enjoyed it this book and learned from it, then I solicit for your help.

Please take a moment of your time
to leave a review for this book on Amazon.

https://www.amazon.com/dp/B07L9GV8XM

ABOUT THE AUTHOR

D r. Richard ONEBAMOI is an apostle by divine calling, an author, a business consultant, a leadership alignment strategist, and a success facilitator. Dr. Onebamoi is the founder and senior pastor of Living Stone World Worship Centre, "One God, One family, One Destiny," located in Brussels, Belgium. Dr. Onebamoi is also a certified coach, speaker, and trainer for The John Maxwell Team. Furthermore, he is the Founder of Men of Visionary Excellence (M.O.V.E).

Dr. Onebamoi is the founder and executive facilitator of The ROCK Consulting Group, with a mandate to inspire your performance, expand your imagination, cultivate your dreams, empower your success, and help you discover, develop, and maximize your God-given potential. He can provide leadership, success, motivation, and educational and positive personal development training that will maximize potentials and minimize liabilities.

A vibrant and charismatic minister and highly sought after conference speaker and published author of several books, including *Success Power Points*, *Kingdom Principles on Leadership*, *Whose Report Will You Believe?*, *Anatomy Of Frustration*, and *Winning Ways for Success*. Dr. Onebamoi carries an apostolic grace upon his life, an anointing to bring changes to the lives of his listeners. He has a profound and unique insight into God's word. As he ministers around the globe, God continually marks his ministry with the demonstration of the Holy Spirit, transforming lives by the Word of His power.

Dr. Onebamoi is happily married to Catherine K. ONEBAMOI, who co-pastors with him and the associate executive facilitator of The ROCK Consulting Group and Richard Onebamoi International (ROI). They are blessed with four children, Naomi-Lisha, Nearia-Destinie, Nathania-Mia, and Nathan-Richard Jr., and they reside in Brussels, Belgium in the heart of the European Union.

Richard Onebamoi welcomes the opportunity to minister in churches, seminars, conventions, retreats, or men's, women's and youth groups. Richard is contacted at:

Richard Onebamoi
P.O. Box 30
1200 Brussels
Belgium
Email: info@richardonebamoi.com
Website: www.richardonebamoi.com
www.richardonebamoibooks.com

www.ingramcontent.com/pod-product-compliance
Lightning Source LLC
LaVergne TN
LVHW011358080426
835511LV00005B/330